MASTERING
KUBERNETES

Deploy, Manage, and Scale Containerized Applications

THOMPSON CARTER

TABLE OF CONTENTS

MASTERING KUBERNETES

INTRODUCTION

1. Welcome to Game Development with Unity

Game development is a fascinating field, one that combines art, storytelling, and technology to create interactive experiences that captivate and entertain people worldwide. Whether it's the feeling of exploring a vast open world, the rush of a fast-paced action game, or the challenge of a strategic puzzle, games have a unique power to engage. This book is here to guide you through the journey of creating games with Unity—a versatile, widely used game development engine that empowers both beginner and advanced developers alike.

In this book, you won't just learn how to use Unity; you'll also gain a deeper understanding of the game development process. We'll approach each topic with real-world examples and practical exercises to ensure that by the end, you're equipped with skills that translate into building your own games, not just replicating examples.

2. Why Unity? Understanding the Game Engine's Power and Flexibility

Unity has become one of the most popular game engines in the world, and for good reason. Unity provides a powerful and intuitive interface, a highly customizable development environment, and support for both 2D and 3D games. Whether you're an indie developer aiming to build a small mobile game or a professional working on a large project, Unity's flexibility makes it an ideal choice.

Here are some key reasons why Unity has been embraced by developers globally:

- **Cross-Platform Compatibility**: Unity supports over 25 platforms, including mobile, desktop, consoles, and VR/AR devices. This flexibility means you can reach a wide audience with minimal extra work.
- **Extensive Asset Store**: The Unity Asset Store provides a vast collection of pre-made assets, tools, and templates, making it easy to add everything from 3D models to special effects.
- **Intuitive Interface**: Unity's interface is designed to be approachable for beginners, yet powerful enough for advanced users. It offers a range of tools for designing, coding, and managing projects.
- **Thriving Community and Support**: With millions of users worldwide, Unity has an active community ready to share tutorials, assets, and advice. This supportive ecosystem ensures help is always available when you need it.

Throughout this book, you'll learn how to leverage these strengths, making Unity's powerful features work for you. By the end, Unity won't just be a tool you use—it will be a platform you understand and feel comfortable with, one that lets you express your creativity.

3. What This Book Covers: Breaking Down Game Development with Real-World Examples

Each chapter in this book builds on the previous one, starting with basic concepts and progressing to more advanced topics. Here's a quick overview of what you can expect:

- **Unity Interface and Setup**: We start with a guided tour of Unity's user interface, helping you become comfortable navigating the various panels and windows. You'll set up your first project and understand the different components that make up a Unity project.
- **Creating Game Worlds**: From adding objects and environments to working with lighting and sound, you'll learn how to bring your game world to life.
- **Scripting with C#**: Unity's scripting language, C#, is essential for creating interactive elements. We'll cover basic programming concepts in a way that's accessible even if you're new to coding.
- **Implementing Game Mechanics**: Game mechanics are the heart of any game. From controlling characters to adding physics, you'll learn to create gameplay that feels responsive and engaging.

- **User Interface (UI) and HUD Design**: A game's user interface guides players and enhances their experience. You'll learn to design intuitive interfaces and displays that provide essential information without distracting from gameplay.
- **Advanced Features**: For those ready to dive deeper, we'll cover multiplayer features, AI programming, and optimization techniques to improve your game's performance.

By using real-world examples—whether it's implementing enemy AI or building a simple inventory system—this book ensures that each chapter gives you practical skills you can apply immediately.

4. Who This Book Is For

This book is designed for anyone interested in learning game development with Unity, regardless of experience level. If you're new to programming or game design, you'll find step-by-step instructions and explanations that make complex concepts easier to understand. For experienced developers, this book will serve as a guide to Unity's advanced features, offering insights into efficient workflows and best practices.

Here's a breakdown of how readers at different levels can benefit:

- **Beginners**: If you've never written a line of code or touched a game engine before, you're in the right place.

Each chapter begins with foundational concepts, progressing gradually to ensure you don't feel overwhelmed.

- **Intermediate Developers**: If you're familiar with some game development concepts, you'll find value in the deeper dives into scripting, optimization, and game mechanics.
- **Experienced Developers**: Even seasoned developers will find Unity-specific insights and advanced workflows useful, especially if they're transitioning from another engine.

5. *What Makes a Great Game? A Look at Core Game Design Principles*

Before diving into Unity, let's consider what makes a game enjoyable. Understanding these core principles will help you design with purpose, aiming to create experiences that resonate with players.

- **Engaging Gameplay**: Successful games have compelling mechanics that keep players engaged, whether it's through challenges, rewards, or freedom to explore.
- **Intuitive Controls**: Games should feel responsive and easy to control, allowing players to focus on the experience rather than struggling with mechanics.
- **Aesthetic Appeal**: While graphics aren't everything, a visually appealing game enhances immersion. Unity's tools can help you create both realistic and stylized visuals.

- **Emotional Connection**: Games often tell stories or present challenges that evoke emotions, whether excitement, fear, or curiosity.

Unity is designed to help you achieve each of these qualities, but it's up to you, the developer, to decide how to bring them together in a way that feels cohesive.

6. The Journey from Idea to Game

Game development is a process. It's not just about learning a set of tools and techniques; it's about understanding how to turn a creative idea into a playable experience. Here are the stages you'll typically go through:

- **Conceptualization**: Defining your game's concept, mechanics, and audience.
- **Prototyping**: Building a basic version to test ideas and refine mechanics.
- **Development**: Building the game world, programming mechanics, and polishing the experience.
- **Testing**: Ensuring the game functions as intended and is enjoyable to play.
- **Publishing**: Releasing your game to the world.

This book follows this journey, providing insights and practical advice at each stage, so that by the end, you'll understand the complete lifecycle of game development.

7. Real-World Examples and Exercises: Hands-On Learning

Theory alone won't make you a skilled game developer. That's why this book emphasizes hands-on learning. In each chapter, you'll find practical exercises that reinforce what you've learned, along with real-world examples to show how professional developers approach similar challenges.

Here's what to expect:

- **Hands-on Exercises**: Step-by-step projects and coding exercises to solidify concepts.
- **Case Studies**: Examples from real games (both big-budget and indie) that illustrate how Unity's tools can be used in diverse ways.
- **Challenges**: At the end of some chapters, you'll find optional challenges designed to test your skills and push your creativity further.

8. Tips for Success and Staying Motivated

Learning game development is a marathon, not a sprint. It can feel overwhelming at times, especially when tackling new concepts or troubleshooting issues. Here are some tips to keep in mind as you work through this book:

- **Start Small**: Don't worry about creating the next blockbuster game immediately. Begin with small projects that focus on specific skills, and build from there.

- **Embrace Mistakes**: Bugs and errors are a natural part of the development process. Each one offers a learning opportunity.
- **Experiment and Explore**: Game development is as much an art as it is a science. Experiment with Unity's features, try new ideas, and don't be afraid to diverge from the book's examples.
- **Seek Feedback**: Show your work to others and listen to their feedback. Fresh eyes can often spot things you've missed.

Game development is both challenging and rewarding. By the end of this book, you'll not only have the skills to create games with Unity, but also the confidence to pursue your own projects and bring your unique ideas to life.

9. Let's Get Started!

Game development with Unity is a skill that will serve you well, whether you're aiming for a career in the industry or simply want to create games for fun. As you begin this journey, remember that learning is a process. Take it one chapter at a time, experiment, and enjoy the process. By the end, you'll have the skills and knowledge to create your own games, as well as the confidence to explore Unity's vast potential on your own.

In the next chapter, we'll start with the basics of Unity's interface and get your first project up and running. Let's dive in!

CHAPTER 1: INTRODUCTION TO KUBERNETES AND CONTAINERIZATION

In this chapter, we'll explore the origins and purpose of Kubernetes, understand the basics of containerization, and learn why Kubernetes has become essential in managing modern applications. We'll also look at real-world examples of Kubernetes in action, and provide a basic guide to setting up Kubernetes on a local machine, preparing us for hands-on practice in the chapters ahead.

Overview of Kubernetes: History, Purpose, and Evolution

1. **The Origin of Kubernetes**:
   - o Kubernetes, often abbreviated as "K8s," was developed by Google in 2014. It originated from Google's internal cluster management system, **Borg**, which allowed Google to manage billions of containers across massive infrastructure. Kubernetes was later open-sourced to help organizations manage large numbers of applications with minimal operational overhead.

2. **Why Kubernetes Exists**:

- o As applications grow, managing them manually becomes challenging, especially when scaling across multiple servers and regions.
- o Kubernetes was designed to automate the deployment, scaling, and management of applications across a distributed environment, offering a way to ensure that services remain available and scalable.

3. **Evolution and Key Milestones**:
   - o Since its open-source release, Kubernetes has become the de facto standard for container orchestration. The **Cloud Native Computing Foundation (CNCF)** adopted Kubernetes to promote its development, leading to widespread adoption by major cloud providers like AWS, Google Cloud, and Azure.

4. **Purpose of Kubernetes**:
   - o Kubernetes simplifies the deployment and scaling of applications, improves resource management, and reduces manual intervention. It enables businesses to **build, deploy, and scale applications reliably and efficiently**, whether they are small startups or large enterprises.

Introduction to Containers: Why Containers are Useful and How They Differ from Virtual Machines

1. **What are Containers?**
   - o A container is a lightweight, standalone package that includes everything needed to run a specific application: code, libraries, dependencies, and runtime.
   - o Containers ensure that applications run consistently across different environments by packaging them in a self-contained format.

2. **Containers vs. Virtual Machines (VMs)**:
   - o **Virtual Machines**: VMs run entire operating systems (OS) alongside the application, making them resource-intensive.
   - o **Containers**: Containers share the host OS kernel, which makes them much lighter, faster to deploy, and easier to scale compared to VMs.
   - o **Comparison**:
     - VMs provide better isolation but require more resources.
     - Containers are lightweight, allow faster startup times, and are ideal for applications that need to be deployed rapidly across environments.

3. **Why Use Containers?**
   - o Containers solve compatibility issues by allowing developers to package applications with all

dependencies, ensuring consistent performance across development, testing, and production.

o Containers enable **microservices architecture**, where applications are broken into smaller, independent services, allowing greater flexibility in development and scaling.

Real-World Applications: Companies and Scenarios Using Kubernetes

1. **Industry Use Cases**:
   o **Tech Giants**: Companies like Google, Spotify, and Twitter use Kubernetes to manage services that support millions of users. Kubernetes allows them to **scale applications dynamically** and ensure high availability.
   o **E-commerce**: Large e-commerce platforms (e.g., Shopify) use Kubernetes to manage spikes in traffic, especially during peak shopping seasons. Kubernetes helps them automatically scale resources based on demand.
   o **Financial Services**: Banks and fintech companies deploy Kubernetes for transaction processing, fraud detection, and customer-facing applications. Kubernetes' high availability and fault tolerance are crucial for these use cases.

- o **Healthcare and Pharmaceuticals**: Organizations use Kubernetes to manage data pipelines, patient data storage, and research applications, ensuring data is accessible but secure.

2. **Benefits in Real-World Scenarios**:

   - o **Cost Savings**: Kubernetes helps companies optimize resource usage, reducing unnecessary overhead by shutting down resources when demand is low.

   - o **Improved Deployment Speed**: Developers can quickly deploy and update applications with minimal downtime, enhancing the development lifecycle.

   - o **Resilience and Reliability**: Kubernetes' self-healing features ensure that applications are highly available, even in the event of hardware or application failure.

3. **Example**:

   - o Imagine an online video streaming service that needs to deliver high-quality video streams to millions of users. Using Kubernetes, the company can deploy multiple instances of video streaming applications across data centers. As demand increases, Kubernetes automatically scales resources to ensure each user receives a consistent, high-quality experience without interruption.

Setting Up Kubernetes: Basic Setup on Local Machines

1. **Local Development with Minikube**:
   - **Minikube** is a tool that allows you to run a single-node Kubernetes cluster on your local machine. It's perfect for testing and learning Kubernetes without needing a full cloud environment.
   - **Installing Minikube**:
     - For Linux/macOS, you can use package managers like Homebrew (brew install minikube) or download Minikube directly from Minikube's GitHub page.
     - For Windows, Minikube is available via Chocolatey or by downloading an installer.

2. **Setting Up Minikube**:
   - **Step 1**: Start Minikube.

     bash
     minikube start

   - **Step 2**: Verify Minikube is running.

bash

Copy code

minikube status

- o **Step 3**: Access the Minikube Dashboard (Optional).

bash

minikube dashboard

  - This opens a web-based interface where you can visually manage and monitor your Kubernetes cluster.

3. **Using kubectl for Cluster Management**:
   - o **kubectl** is the command-line tool used to interact with Kubernetes clusters. It is essential for managing deployments, services, and other Kubernetes resources.
   - o **Installing kubectl**:
     - Install kubectl by following the instructions from the Kubernetes documentation.
   - o **Basic kubectl Commands**:
     - **Check cluster nodes**:

bash

kubectl get nodes

     - **Deploy a sample application**:

bash

kubectl create deployment hello-minikube --
image=k8s.gcr.io/echoserver:1.4

- **Expose the application to the outside world**:

bash

kubectl expose deployment hello-minikube -
-type=NodePort --port=8080

- **Access the application**:

bash

minikube service hello-minikube

4. **Sample Application Deployment on Minikube**:
   - To get hands-on with Kubernetes, deploy a simple web server application that displays a welcome message. This application will serve as our first test and give you experience with kubectl commands and Minikube.
   - **Steps**:
     - **Step 1**: Start Minikube as described above.
     - **Step 2**: Deploy the application.

     bash

```
kubectl create deployment my-webapp --
image=nginx
```

- **Step 3**: Expose the application to access it from your local machine.

```
bash
kubectl expose deployment my-webapp --
type=NodePort --port=80
```

- **Step 4**: Get the URL to access the application.

```
bash
minikube service my-webapp --url
```

- **Step 5**: Open the URL in your browser to view your first Kubernetes-managed application!

5. **Stopping and Deleting Minikube**:
   o When you're finished, stop Minikube to free up resources:

```
bash
minikube stop
```

   o To delete the Minikube cluster entirely:

```bash
minikube delete
```

In this introductory chapter, we covered the essentials of Kubernetes and containerization. We looked at the history and purpose of Kubernetes, the role of containers, and the advantages they provide over traditional virtual machines. By examining real-world applications of Kubernetes, we saw how organizations of all sizes leverage Kubernetes for efficiency, scalability, and reliability. Finally, we walked through the basic steps to set up Kubernetes on a local machine using Minikube, setting the stage for more advanced concepts and hands-on practice in the upcoming chapters.

In the next chapter, we'll explore Kubernetes' architecture in detail, examining how its components work together to manage and deploy applications seamlessly.

CHAPTER 2: KUBERNETES ARCHITECTURE ESSENTIALS

Kubernetes has a unique architecture that enables it to manage applications effectively across multiple nodes, ensuring high availability, scalability, and fault tolerance. In this chapter, we'll explore the core components of Kubernetes, understand the roles of essential components like the kube-apiserver, etcd, kube-scheduler, and kube-controller-manager, and see how Kubernetes manages resources using a real-world analogy.

Core Components: Nodes, Clusters, Pods, and the Control Plane

1. **Clusters**:
   o A **Kubernetes cluster** is a group of machines—physical or virtual—that work together to manage and run containerized applications. A cluster comprises **nodes** that host applications, managed by the **control plane**, which coordinates tasks across the cluster.

- o Think of a Kubernetes cluster as a "mini data center" capable of running multiple applications while maintaining organization, load balancing, and resource allocation.

2. **Nodes**:

- o A **node** is a machine (virtual or physical) in a Kubernetes cluster where applications are deployed. Each node contains the resources necessary to run one or more **pods** and is managed by the control plane.
- o **Node Components**:
  - **kubelet**: The agent on each node that communicates with the control plane and ensures containers are running as expected.
  - **kube-proxy**: Manages network rules on the node, enabling communication between different pods across the cluster.
- o Nodes are the "workhorses" of Kubernetes. They carry out instructions from the control plane and ensure that applications run seamlessly.

3. **Pods**:

- o A **pod** is the smallest deployable unit in Kubernetes and represents one or more containers working together as a single entity. Containers in a pod share the same network namespace and storage resources, making it possible for them to communicate and function as one application.

- o **Single vs. Multi-Container Pods**:
  - **Single-container pods**: Ideal for simple applications where each pod runs a single instance.
  - **Multi-container pods**: Useful when containers need to share resources closely (e.g., a web server and a log processor).
- o Pods are ephemeral, meaning they can be terminated or restarted based on demand or in case of failure, allowing Kubernetes to maintain a healthy application environment.

4. **Control Plane**:
  - o The **control plane** is the "brain" of Kubernetes. It manages nodes, schedules workloads, and maintains the desired state of applications within the cluster.
  - o Components of the control plane (e.g., kube-apiserver, etcd) operate together to handle complex tasks like scheduling, maintaining state, and coordinating deployments.

Roles of Key Components: Understanding kube-apiserver, etcd, kube-scheduler, and kube-controller-manager

1. **kube-apiserver**:

- o The **kube-apiserver** is the central API server that acts as a communication hub within Kubernetes. It receives instructions from users (through kubectl), validates requests, and serves as the entry point for all interactions with the control plane.
- o The kube-apiserver also enforces access control and data validation, ensuring that all data is consistent and secure.

2. **etcd**:

- o **etcd** is a distributed key-value store that acts as Kubernetes' "brain." It stores all configuration data, states, and metadata for the entire cluster. This includes information about nodes, pods, configurations, and network settings.
- o **High Availability**: etcd's distributed nature ensures data is replicated across multiple nodes, so Kubernetes maintains its desired state even if a node fails.
- o Think of etcd as the "memory" of the cluster, where critical information is stored and retrieved, helping Kubernetes track the current state of the system.

3. **kube-scheduler**:

- o The **kube-scheduler** is responsible for placing pods on nodes. It monitors resource requirements, availability, and constraints to determine the best

making it possible for them to communicate and function as one application.

- o **Single vs. Multi-Container Pods**:
  - ▪ **Single-container pods**: Ideal for simple applications where each pod runs a single instance.
  - ▪ **Multi-container pods**: Useful when containers need to share resources closely (e.g., a web server and a log processor).
- o Pods are ephemeral, meaning they can be terminated or restarted based on demand or in case of failure, allowing Kubernetes to maintain a healthy application environment.

4. **Control Plane**:
   - o The **control plane** is the "brain" of Kubernetes. It manages nodes, schedules workloads, and maintains the desired state of applications within the cluster.
   - o Components of the control plane (e.g., kube-apiserver, etcd) operate together to handle complex tasks like scheduling, maintaining state, and coordinating deployments.

Roles of Key Components: Understanding kube-apiserver, etcd, kube-scheduler, and kube-controller-manager

1. **kube-apiserver**:

o The **kube-apiserver** is the central API server that acts as a communication hub within Kubernetes. It receives instructions from users (through kubectl), validates requests, and serves as the entry point for all interactions with the control plane.

o The kube-apiserver also enforces access control and data validation, ensuring that all data is consistent and secure.

2. **etcd**:

o **etcd** is a distributed key-value store that acts as Kubernetes' "brain." It stores all configuration data, states, and metadata for the entire cluster. This includes information about nodes, pods, configurations, and network settings.

o **High Availability**: etcd's distributed nature ensures data is replicated across multiple nodes, so Kubernetes maintains its desired state even if a node fails.

o Think of etcd as the "memory" of the cluster, where critical information is stored and retrieved, helping Kubernetes track the current state of the system.

3. **kube-scheduler**:

o The **kube-scheduler** is responsible for placing pods on nodes. It monitors resource requirements, availability, and constraints to determine the best node for each pod, ensuring efficient resource usage across the cluster.

- o The scheduler considers factors like CPU, memory, and network availability, prioritizing nodes that can handle the pod's needs while balancing load.

4. **kube-controller-manager**:

- o The **kube-controller-manager** is a collection of controllers that maintain the cluster's desired state by managing objects like deployments, endpoints, and replicas.

- o **Key Controllers**:

  - **Replication controller**: Ensures the specified number of pod replicas are running.

  - **Node controller**: Monitors node health and manages node failure responses.

  - **Service controller**: Manages load balancing and network endpoints for services.

- o The kube-controller-manager is like the "control center" of Kubernetes, ensuring each aspect of the cluster's desired state is met and intervening when needed.

How Kubernetes Manages Resources: Real-World Analogy for Resource Allocation

1. **Resource Requests and Limits**:

- **Requests**: The minimum amount of resources (CPU, memory) a container needs to run effectively.
- **Limits**: The maximum amount of resources a container is allowed to use. Kubernetes enforces these limits to prevent applications from consuming too many resources and affecting other applications.

2. **Real-World Analogy for Resource Allocation**:
   - Imagine Kubernetes as a hotel with rooms (nodes) and guests (pods). Each guest has specific requirements for room size and amenities. The hotel manager (kube-scheduler) checks available rooms and assigns a room that fits each guest's needs without overbooking.
   - **Requests and Limits**: Just like each guest needs a minimum room size (request) and has a maximum allowance for room features (limit), Kubernetes allocates minimum and maximum resources to ensure each pod gets the necessary resources without overcrowding the cluster.

3. **Namespace for Resource Isolation**:
   - **Namespaces** allow Kubernetes to divide cluster resources between multiple users or teams, providing isolated environments.
   - Think of namespaces as different floors in the hotel, each dedicated to a different group of guests. Each

floor (namespace) has its own rules, services, and amenities, allowing multiple groups to coexist without interfering with each other.

4. **Kubernetes' Self-Healing Capabilities**:

   o Kubernetes monitors applications and automatically restarts failed pods, replaces unresponsive nodes, and reassigns pods to healthy nodes to maintain uptime and availability.

   o This self-healing feature ensures that applications remain available, even if individual nodes or containers fail.

Example Scenario: A Kubernetes Deployment in Action

Let's consider a simple web application that serves dynamic content to thousands of users. Here's how Kubernetes components work together to ensure the application's reliability, scalability, and efficiency:

1. **Application Deployment**:

   o The application is containerized, and a YAML configuration file defines the deployment settings (e.g., image, replicas, resource requests).

   o The user submits the deployment request to the kube-apiserver, which validates it and stores the desired state in etcd.

2. **Pod Scheduling**:
   - The kube-scheduler reviews resource requirements, checks node availability, and assigns the application's pods to nodes with sufficient resources.

3. **Maintaining Desired State**:
   - The kube-controller-manager ensures the specified number of pod replicas are running. If a pod fails, the controller creates a replacement to match the desired state.

4. **Load Balancing**:
   - A service is set up to expose the application to external users. The kube-proxy on each node handles network rules to direct traffic evenly across pod replicas, ensuring users experience consistent response times.

5. **Resource Management and Self-Healing**:
   - Kubernetes continuously monitors the application's CPU and memory usage, scaling resources up or down based on demand.
   - If a node becomes unresponsive, Kubernetes reschedules the application's pods to healthy nodes, maintaining uptime and availability for users.

In this chapter, we delved into the essential components of Kubernetes and how they interact to create a reliable and efficient container orchestration system. We covered the core components—clusters, nodes, pods, and the control plane—and examined the roles of the kube-apiserver, etcd, kube-scheduler, and kube-controller-manager in maintaining the cluster's desired state. Finally, we used a real-world analogy to explain Kubernetes' approach to resource management, making these abstract concepts easier to understand.

In the next chapter, we'll put this knowledge into practice by setting up our first Kubernetes cluster, deploying applications, and exploring hands-on examples to reinforce these foundational concepts.

CHAPTER 3: SETTING UP YOUR FIRST KUBERNETES CLUSTER

Setting up a Kubernetes cluster for the first time can be a challenging yet exciting step in mastering container orchestration. This chapter explores different ways to install Kubernetes, provides a step-by-step guide for setting up a local Kubernetes cluster with Minikube, and walks through configuring a simple web application to run on Kubernetes. By the end of this chapter, you'll have a basic but functional Kubernetes environment and be ready to start experimenting with deploying containerized applications.

Kubernetes Installation Options: Minikube, Kind, and Cloud Providers

There are several ways to set up a Kubernetes cluster, depending on your goals, environment, and resources.

1. **Minikube**:
    - **Purpose**: Minikube is a lightweight tool that runs a single-node Kubernetes cluster on your local machine. It's ideal for learning and development since it doesn't require complex infrastructure.

- o **Best for**: Beginners who want to experiment with Kubernetes without the cost of cloud resources. Minikube includes features like load balancing, container runtime integration, and a dashboard.
- o **Limitations**: Since it's a single-node cluster, it's not suitable for high-availability or production-level workloads.

2. **Kind (Kubernetes in Docker)**:
   - o **Purpose**: Kind allows you to run Kubernetes clusters inside Docker containers. It's useful for running multi-node clusters locally, making it a great option for development, testing, and CI/CD pipelines.
   - o **Best for**: Developers who need multi-node configurations and want the flexibility of Docker-based clusters.
   - o **Limitations**: Limited to local environments and lacks some advanced features of cloud-based or production-grade clusters.

3. **Cloud Providers (GKE, EKS, AKS)**:
   - o **Purpose**: Most major cloud providers, including Google Kubernetes Engine (GKE), Amazon Elastic Kubernetes Service (EKS), and Azure Kubernetes Service (AKS), offer managed Kubernetes services. These services automate much of the cluster setup

and management, providing scalability, high availability, and access to advanced features.

- o **Best for**: Production workloads or applications requiring scaling, reliability, and global availability.
- o **Limitations**: Managed services can be costly, especially if you're experimenting or learning.

Launching a Cluster Locally: Step-by-Step Guide to Setting Up Minikube

For this tutorial, we'll focus on **Minikube**, a popular choice for setting up a local Kubernetes cluster. Minikube is beginner-friendly and allows us to explore Kubernetes fundamentals without needing cloud infrastructure.

Prerequisites:

- **Hardware**: Minikube requires at least 2GB of RAM and 2 CPUs.
- **Software**: You'll need a container or virtual machine manager (e.g., Docker or VirtualBox) to host the cluster.

Step 1: Install Minikube

1. **Linux/macOS**: Install Minikube using curl.

   bash
   Copy code

```
curl                                          -LO
https://storage.googleapis.com/minikube/releases/latest/min
ikube-linux-amd64
sudo install minikube-linux-amd64 /usr/local/bin/minikube
```

2. **Windows**: Download Minikube from Minikube's GitHub releases and install it.

3. **Verify the Installation**:

```
bash
Copy code
minikube version
```

Step 2: Install kubectl

kubectl is the command-line tool that allows us to interact with Kubernetes clusters.

1. **Install kubectl**:
   - On Linux/macOS:

```
bash
Copy code
curl                                          -LO
"https://storage.googleapis.com/kubernetes-
release/release/$(curl                        -s
https://storage.googleapis.com/kubernetes-
release/release/stable.txt)/bin/linux/amd64/kubectl"
```

chmod +x ./kubectl

sudo mv ./kubectl /usr/local/bin/kubectl

o   On Windows, follow instructions from the official
    Kubernetes documentation.

2. **Verify the Installation**:

bash

Copy code

kubectl version --client

Step 3: Start Minikube

1. **Start the Cluster**:

    o   Run the following command to start Minikube:

    bash

    Copy code

    minikube start

    o   Minikube will automatically detect your container
        or VM manager (Docker, VirtualBox, etc.) and
        create a single-node cluster.

2. **Check Minikube Status**:

    o   After Minikube starts, check the status to verify that
        everything is running as expected:

    bash

Copy code

minikube status

3. **Access the Minikube Dashboard**:

   o Minikube provides a web-based dashboard that allows you to visualize and manage the cluster:

   bash

   Copy code

   minikube dashboard

   o The dashboard opens in a browser and provides a graphical interface for viewing nodes, pods, deployments, and more.

Step 4: Verify the Cluster

1. **Check Cluster Nodes**:

   o Run the following command to see the nodes in your cluster:

   bash

   Copy code

   kubectl get nodes

   o You should see a single node in the Ready state, indicating that the Minikube cluster is functioning.

2. **Check Cluster Information**:
   - ○ Get additional details about the cluster using:

   bash

   Copy code

   kubectl cluster-info

   - ○ This command provides the URLs of key services like the API server and DNS.

Real-World Example: Configuring a Simple Web Application to Run on Kubernetes

Now that we have a running Minikube cluster, let's deploy a simple web application to see how Kubernetes manages containers and services.

Step 1: Create a Deployment

1. **Define the Deployment**:
   - ○ Use kubectl to create a deployment for a simple **nginx** web server.

   bash

   Copy code

   kubectl create deployment web-server --image=nginx

2. **Verify the Deployment**:
   - ○ Check the status of the deployment:

```bash
Copy code
kubectl get deployments
```

- ○ You should see the **web-server** deployment with one replica, which Kubernetes automatically schedules on the Minikube node.

Step 2: Expose the Deployment as a Service

To access the web server from outside the cluster, we need to expose it using a Kubernetes **Service**.

1. **Expose the Deployment**:
   - ○ Run the following command to create a **NodePort** service that opens a port on the Minikube node:

```bash
Copy code
kubectl expose deployment web-server --
type=NodePort --port=80
```

2. **Get Service Information**:
   - ○ Check the details of the newly created service:

```bash
Copy code
kubectl get services
```

- The output shows a list of services, including web-server, with a NodePort type, which provides a port number (e.g., 30000-32767) that can be used to access the service externally.

Step 3: Access the Application

1. **Access the Application through Minikube**:
   - Use the following command to get a direct URL to access the web-server service:

     bash
     Copy code
     minikube service web-server --url

   - This command returns a URL (e.g., http://192.168.99.100:31245) that you can open in a browser to view the nginx welcome page, confirming that your application is successfully running on Kubernetes.

2. **Verify Application Pods**:
   - To see the pods that are running the nginx web server, use:

     bash
     Copy code
     kubectl get pods

o The output lists each pod created by the web-server deployment, showing its status as Running.

Step 4: Scale the Application (Optional)

Kubernetes makes it easy to scale applications up or down based on demand.

1. **Scale Up the Deployment**:

   o Increase the number of web-server replicas to 3:

   bash

   Copy code

   kubectl scale deployment web-server --replicas=3

2. **Verify the Pods**:

   o Check that additional pods were created:

   bash

   Copy code

   kubectl get pods

   o You should now see three pods running the nginx web server, each managed by Kubernetes to ensure they remain in a Running state.

3. **Testing Load Balancing**:

   o Kubernetes will automatically balance traffic between the three pods in the web-server deployment. This simple example illustrates Kubernetes' ability to scale applications and distribute requests across multiple replicas for better reliability.

Stopping and Cleaning Up Minikube

1. **Stop Minikube**:
   - o To stop the Minikube cluster:

   bash
   Copy code
   minikube stop

2. **Delete the Minikube Cluster**:
   - o If you no longer need the cluster and want to free up resources, you can delete it:

   bash
   Copy code
   minikube delete

In this chapter, we explored different ways to set up Kubernetes, from local solutions like Minikube and Kind to managed cloud providers. We then provided a detailed, step-by-step guide to setting up Minikube, including installing required tools like kubectl. Finally, we walked through deploying a simple web application, exposing it as a service, and scaling it to handle increased demand.

You now have a functional Kubernetes environment and a solid understanding of basic deployment processes. In the next chapter, we'll dive into more advanced deployment techniques,

CHAPTER 4: DEPLOYING APPLICATIONS ON KUBERNETES

Deploying applications is one of the primary functions of Kubernetes, and it all starts with understanding the core building blocks of Kubernetes: **pods** and **containers**. This chapter covers the essentials of deploying applications on Kubernetes, including creating and managing deployments using YAML files, and explores Kubernetes' powerful scaling and self-healing features with real-world scenarios

Working with Pods and Containers: Understanding the Building Blocks

1. **Containers**:
    - **Containers** are lightweight, self-contained runtime environments that include an application and all its dependencies. They are isolated from other applications but share the host OS, making them efficient and fast to deploy.
    - Containers are created from **images** (like Docker images), which define the application code, system libraries, and environment required to run the application.

2. **Pods**:
   - A **pod** is the smallest deployable unit in Kubernetes, representing one or more containers that share the same network and storage resources. Containers within a pod are tightly coupled and work together as a single entity.
   - **Single vs. Multi-Container Pods**:
     - **Single-Container Pod**: The most common pod setup, where a single container is managed by a pod. Ideal for simple applications.
     - **Multi-Container Pod**: Useful when two or more containers need to work closely together. For example, a web server and a logging container that processes server logs can be placed in the same pod.
   - **Pod Lifecycle**:
     - Pods are ephemeral by nature, meaning they can be created, replaced, or terminated based on demand or availability. Kubernetes manages pods automatically to ensure that applications stay available and are quickly restarted in case of failure.
3. **Using kubectl to Create and Manage Pods**:

o To experiment with pods, let's create a simple pod running an nginx web server directly using kubectl.

```bash
Copy code
kubectl run my-pod --image=nginx --restart=Never
```

o Check the status of the pod:

```bash
Copy code
kubectl get pods
```

o This command shows the pod's name, status, and other details. However, this is mainly for testing. In practice, we'll use **deployments** to manage pods.

Creating and Managing Deployments: A Hands-On Example with YAML

1. **What is a Deployment?**
   o A **deployment** is a Kubernetes resource that provides declarative updates for pods and replica sets. Deployments allow you to define the desired state of an application, including the number of replicas, update strategies, and rolling updates.

o Deployments automate the process of creating, scaling, and managing multiple replicas of pods to keep your applications available and up-to-date.

2. **Writing a Deployment YAML File**:

o YAML files are the preferred way to define and manage Kubernetes resources, making it easy to version control configurations.

o Below is a YAML file for a simple nginx deployment:

```yaml
Copy code
apiVersion: apps/v1
kind: Deployment
metadata:
  name: nginx-deployment
  labels:
    app: nginx
spec:
  replicas: 3
  selector:
    matchLabels:
      app: nginx
  template:
    metadata:
      labels:
```

```
      app: nginx
    spec:
      containers:
      - name: nginx
        image: nginx:1.14.2
        ports:
        - containerPort: 80
```

3. **Understanding the Deployment YAML File**:
   - **apiVersion**: Specifies the API version of the deployment resource (e.g., apps/v1).
   - **kind**: The type of Kubernetes object being created, which in this case is a **Deployment**.
   - **metadata**: Defines metadata for the deployment, such as name and labels.
   - **spec**: The deployment specification, including:
     - **replicas**: The desired number of pod replicas.
     - **selector**: Defines the labels used to match pods.
     - **template**: Describes the pod template, including the pod's metadata and specifications for containers within the pod.

4. **Deploying the Application**:
   - Save the YAML file as nginx-deployment.yaml and apply it using kubectl:

bash

Copy code

kubectl apply -f nginx-deployment.yaml

o   Check the status of the deployment:

bash

Copy code

kubectl get deployments

o   View the running pods:

bash

Copy code

kubectl get pods -l app=nginx

5. **Updating a Deployment**:

o   To update the deployment (e.g., upgrading the nginx version), edit the YAML file, change the image version, and reapply it:

yaml

Copy code

Updated container image in nginx-deployment.yaml

image: nginx:1.16.1

o Apply the update:

```bash
Copy code
kubectl apply -f nginx-deployment.yaml
```

o Kubernetes will perform a **rolling update**, replacing each pod one by one to ensure no downtime.

6. **Deleting a Deployment**:
   o To delete the deployment and associated pods:

```bash
Copy code
kubectl delete -f nginx-deployment.yaml
```

Scaling and Self-Healing: Real-World Scenario of Autoscaling Under High Demand

Kubernetes supports scaling and self-healing out-of-the-box, ensuring that applications can handle increased load and recover from failures automatically.

1. **Scaling Deployments**:
   o Scaling allows Kubernetes to add or remove pod replicas based on demand, ensuring sufficient resources are available during peak times and releasing resources when demand is low.

2. **Horizontal Pod Autoscaler (HPA)**:
   o Kubernetes' **Horizontal Pod Autoscaler** automatically adjusts the number of pod replicas based on resource utilization, typically CPU or memory usage.
   o **Setting Up HPA**:

   bash
   Copy code
   kubectl autoscale deployment nginx-deployment --cpu-percent=50 --min=1 --max=5

   o This command sets up an HPA for the nginx-deployment, instructing Kubernetes to maintain CPU usage around 50% and scaling the replicas between 1 and 5 based on demand.

3. **Monitoring the Autoscaler**:
   o Check the status of the HPA:

   bash
   Copy code
   kubectl get hpa

   o Kubernetes will add or remove replicas as needed, based on the CPU load. This is particularly useful in scenarios where traffic spikes are unpredictable.

4. **Self-Healing Capabilities**:

- o Kubernetes continually monitors pods to ensure they are in a healthy state. If a pod fails, Kubernetes automatically replaces it with a new one, maintaining the desired state.
- o **Real-World Scenario**:
  - Consider an e-commerce site that experiences high traffic during promotions. As traffic increases, Kubernetes' autoscaler adds replicas to handle the load. If a node fails, Kubernetes immediately reschedules the application's pods to healthy nodes, ensuring uninterrupted service.

5. **Using Probes for Health Checks**:
   - o Kubernetes uses **liveness** and **readiness probes** to determine if a pod is running properly and ready to serve requests.
   - o **Example of Liveness and Readiness Probes**:

yaml

Copy code

```
spec:
  containers:
  - name: nginx
    image: nginx:1.14.2
    livenessProbe:
      httpGet:
```

```
        path: /
        port: 80
      initialDelaySeconds: 5
      periodSeconds: 10
    readinessProbe:
    httpGet:
      path: /
      port: 80
      initialDelaySeconds: 5
      periodSeconds: 10
```

- o **livenessProbe**: Kubernetes will restart the pod if it fails this check.
- o **readinessProbe**: Used to determine if the pod is ready to serve traffic. If the probe fails, the pod will be temporarily removed from the load balancer until it's healthy again.

6. **Testing the Autoscaling and Self-Healing**:
    - o You can simulate high demand by increasing CPU or memory usage in the container, triggering the HPA to scale up the deployment. Similarly, you can manually delete a pod and watch Kubernetes automatically create a new one to maintain the desired replica count.

In this chapter, we explored the foundational elements of deploying applications on Kubernetes. We discussed the building blocks of Kubernetes—pods and containers—and learned to create and manage deployments using YAML configuration files. Additionally, we examined Kubernetes' scaling and self-healing features, including the Horizontal Pod Autoscaler and liveness and readiness probes, with a real-world scenario demonstrating how Kubernetes ensures applications stay resilient and responsive to demand.

In the next chapter, we'll dive into services and networking, discovering how Kubernetes enables communication between applications and exposes them to external users.

CHAPTER 5: SERVICES AND NETWORKING IN KUBERNETES

Networking is at the core of Kubernetes, enabling communication between various components and making applications accessible to users. Kubernetes provides different types of **services** to expose applications within the cluster and to the outside world. In this chapter, we'll discuss **ClusterIP**, **NodePort**, and **LoadBalancer** services, delve into Kubernetes' internal DNS system, and walk through a practical example of setting up a service to access an application from outside the cluster.

Exposing Applications: ClusterIP, NodePort, and LoadBalancer Services

In Kubernetes, a **Service** is an abstraction that defines a logical set of pods and provides a stable endpoint to access them. Services ensure that applications remain accessible even if pods are added, removed, or replaced.

1. **ClusterIP (Internal-Only Service)**:
   - **Purpose**: ClusterIP is the default type of service and provides an internal IP address that is only accessible within the cluster. It allows pods and services within the same cluster to communicate without exposing them externally.
   - **Use Case**: Useful for internal services, like databases or APIs that only need to be accessed by other applications within the cluster.
   - **Example**: Setting up a ClusterIP service for an internal API.

   ```yaml
   yaml
   apiVersion: v1
   kind: Service
   metadata:
     name: internal-api
   spec:
     selector:
       app: api
     ports:
       - protocol: TCP
         port: 80
         targetPort: 8080
     type: ClusterIP
   ```

2. **NodePort (External Access Through Node IP)**:

   o **Purpose**: A NodePort service exposes the application on a specific port (between 30000-32767) on each node in the cluster, allowing external traffic to access the application by connecting to <NodeIP>:<NodePort>.

   o **Use Case**: Useful for testing services locally or providing external access without using a load balancer.

   o **Example**: Exposing an application on a NodePort.

```yaml
yaml
apiVersion: v1
kind: Service
metadata:
  name: web-app
spec:
  selector:
    app: web
  ports:
    - protocol: TCP
      port: 80
      targetPort: 8080
      nodePort: 31000
  type: NodePort
```

o In this example, the application will be accessible on port 31000 of each node's IP address.

3. **LoadBalancer (External Access Through Load Balancer)**:

o **Purpose**: A LoadBalancer service creates an external load balancer (if supported by the cloud provider), automatically distributing traffic across multiple nodes and providing a single external IP.

o **Use Case**: Ideal for production applications where you need a stable IP for users to access, often in cloud environments like AWS, GCP, or Azure.

o **Example**: Exposing an application through a LoadBalancer.

yaml
Copy code

```yaml
apiVersion: v1
kind: Service
metadata:
  name: public-web-app
spec:
  selector:
    app: web
  ports:
    - protocol: TCP
      port: 80
```

2. **NodePort (External Access Through Node IP)**:

- ○ **Purpose**: A NodePort service exposes the application on a specific port (between 30000-32767) on each node in the cluster, allowing external traffic to access the application by connecting to <NodeIP>:<NodePort>.

- ○ **Use Case**: Useful for testing services locally or providing external access without using a load balancer.

- ○ **Example**: Exposing an application on a NodePort.

```yaml
apiVersion: v1
kind: Service
metadata:
  name: web-app
spec:
  selector:
    app: web
  ports:
    - protocol: TCP
      port: 80
      targetPort: 8080
      nodePort: 31000
  type: NodePort
```

- o In this example, the application will be accessible on port 31000 of each node's IP address.

3. **LoadBalancer (External Access Through Load Balancer)**:

  - o **Purpose**: A LoadBalancer service creates an external load balancer (if supported by the cloud provider), automatically distributing traffic across multiple nodes and providing a single external IP.

  - o **Use Case**: Ideal for production applications where you need a stable IP for users to access, often in cloud environments like AWS, GCP, or Azure.

  - o **Example**: Exposing an application through a LoadBalancer.

```yaml
Copy code
apiVersion: v1
kind: Service
metadata:
  name: public-web-app
spec:
  selector:
    app: web
  ports:
    - protocol: TCP
      port: 80
```

targetPort: 8080

type: LoadBalancer

- o In this configuration, Kubernetes requests a cloud provider to provision a load balancer and assign a public IP address, making the application accessible to users from the internet.

DNS in Kubernetes: How Kubernetes Uses DNS to Enable Internal Communication

1. **Kubernetes DNS Overview**:
   - o Kubernetes includes an internal DNS service, which automatically assigns DNS names to all services. This allows applications and services to communicate by name instead of IP address, which is especially useful in dynamic environments where pods and IP addresses change frequently.
   - o The DNS naming convention is typically service-name.namespace.svc.cluster.local.

2. **DNS Example**:
   - o If you have a service named db in the default namespace, other services within the cluster can access it using db.default.svc.cluster.local.
   - o Applications don't need to know the IP address of the service; they simply connect using the service's

DNS name, and Kubernetes handles the underlying resolution.

3. **Internal Service Communication**:

   o Kubernetes DNS is crucial for **microservices architectures**, where different components of an application (e.g., API server, database, front end) need to communicate with each other reliably.

   o **Example**: An API service can connect to a database by addressing db-service.default.svc.cluster.local, and Kubernetes DNS resolves the name to the database service's IP address.

4. **Using DNS with ClusterIP Services**:

   o Since ClusterIP services are internal, they depend heavily on Kubernetes DNS. For example, if a frontend service needs to connect to an internal API, it can simply use the API's service name, and Kubernetes will route the traffic correctly.

   o **Benefits**:

      ▪ Simplifies communication between services.

      ▪ Makes services more resilient to IP changes within the cluster.

      ▪ Provides an easy way to organize and scale microservices.

Practical Example: Setting Up a Service to Access Your Application from Outside the Cluster

Let's walk through deploying a simple web application (nginx) and setting it up so it's accessible externally using a NodePort service. This example will help reinforce how to expose services in Kubernetes.

Step 1: Create a Deployment

1. **Define the Deployment**:
   - Use the following YAML file to define a deployment for an nginx web server.

     yaml
     apiVersion: apps/v1
     kind: Deployment
     metadata:
       name: nginx-deployment
     spec:
       replicas: 2
       selector:
         matchLabels:
           app: nginx
       template:
         metadata:
           labels:
             app: nginx
         spec:

```
containers:
- name: nginx
  image: nginx:1.14.2
  ports:
  - containerPort: 80
```

2. **Deploy the Application**:

   o Save the file as nginx-deployment.yaml and deploy it using kubectl:

   ```bash
   kubectl apply -f nginx-deployment.yaml
   ```

   o Verify the deployment by checking the status of the pods:

   ```bash
   kubectl get pods -l app=nginx
   ```

Step 2: Expose the Deployment with a NodePort Service

1. **Define the Service**:

   o To make the nginx application accessible from outside the cluster, create a NodePort service.

   ```yaml
   apiVersion: v1
   kind: Service
   ```

```
metadata:
  name: nginx-service
spec:
  selector:
    app: nginx
  ports:
    - protocol: TCP
      port: 80
      targetPort: 80
      nodePort: 31000
  type: NodePort
```

2. **Deploy the Service**:

   o Save the file as nginx-service.yaml and apply it:

   bash
   kubectl apply -f nginx-service.yaml

   o Check the service's status and assigned NodePort:

   bash
   kubectl get service nginx-service

   o You should see that the nginx-service has a NodePort assigned (e.g., 31000).

Step 3: Access the Application from Outside the Cluster

1. **Find the Node IP**:

    o For a Minikube setup, you can use the following command to get the Minikube IP address:

    bash
    Copy code
    minikube ip

2. **Access the Application**:

    o Open a browser or use curl to access the application using the Node IP and NodePort:

    bash
    Copy code
    curl http://<Minikube-IP>:31000

    o If the setup is correct, you should see the nginx welcome page, confirming that your application is now accessible from outside the cluster.

In this chapter, we explored how Kubernetes services enable networking within the cluster and expose applications externally. We discussed the main service types—**ClusterIP**, **NodePort**, and **LoadBalancer**—and when to use each based on application needs. We also examined how Kubernetes DNS simplifies internal service communication, making it possible to address services by name rather than IP. Finally, we walked through a practical example of deploying a web application, exposing it through a NodePort service, and accessing it from outside the cluster.

In the next chapter, we'll cover **ConfigMaps and Secrets**, which allow you to decouple application configurations and manage sensitive data securely within Kubernetes.

CHAPTER 6: CONFIGMAPS AND SECRETS

Managing configurations and sensitive information is crucial for any application, especially in dynamic environments like Kubernetes. **ConfigMaps** and **Secrets** are Kubernetes resources designed to help you decouple configurations from your application code, making deployments more flexible and secure. In this chapter, we'll cover the purpose of ConfigMaps, best practices for handling sensitive data with Secrets, and a practical example of using both to manage environment variables for an application.

Decoupling Configurations: The Purpose and Advantages of Using ConfigMaps

1. **What is a ConfigMap?**
    - A **ConfigMap** is a Kubernetes object that stores key-value pairs or configuration files used by applications. Instead of hardcoding configurations within container images, ConfigMaps enable you to inject configurations at runtime.
    - ConfigMaps are ideal for storing non-sensitive configuration data, such as environment variables, configuration files, or command-line arguments.

2. **Why Use ConfigMaps?**

   o **Separation of Concerns**: ConfigMaps allow you to separate application code from configurations, which makes your container images more reusable and easier to manage.

   o **Flexibility**: With ConfigMaps, you can update configurations without rebuilding container images or redeploying applications. This is particularly useful for adjusting settings in development, testing, and production environments.

   o **Consistency Across Environments**: ConfigMaps provide a standardized way to manage configurations across Kubernetes clusters, making it easier to maintain consistency between staging, production, and other environments.

3. **Creating a ConfigMap**:

   o You can create a ConfigMap using a YAML file or directly with kubectl.

   o **Example**: Creating a ConfigMap for a web application with environment variables for configuration.

   ```yaml
   Copy code
   apiVersion: v1
   kind: ConfigMap
   ```

```
metadata:
  name: app-config
data:
  APP_NAME: "MyApp"
  LOG_LEVEL: "INFO"
  DATABASE_URL:
"mysql://db_user@db_host/db_name"
```

- o Apply the ConfigMap to the cluster:

```bash
Copy code
kubectl apply -f app-config.yaml
```

4. **Using ConfigMaps in Pods**:

- o Once created, ConfigMaps can be used by pods as environment variables or as configuration files.
- o **Example of using ConfigMap as environment variables** in a deployment:

```yaml
Copy code
apiVersion: apps/v1
kind: Deployment
metadata:
  name: app-deployment
spec:
```

```
      replicas: 2
      selector:
       matchLabels:
        app: myapp
      template:
       metadata:
        labels:
         app: myapp
       spec:
        containers:
        - name: app-container
          image: myapp:latest
          envFrom:
          - configMapRef:
             name: app-config
```

- o In this example, APP_NAME, LOG_LEVEL, and DATABASE_URL will be available as environment variables within each container in the pod.

Managing Sensitive Data with Secrets: Best Practices for Security

1. **What is a Secret?**

- A **Secret** is a Kubernetes object used to store sensitive information, such as API keys, passwords, or TLS certificates. Secrets ensure that sensitive data is managed securely and isn't exposed within container images or in the application code.

2. **Why Use Secrets?**

- **Security**: Secrets are stored in base64-encoded format, making them more secure than plaintext. They can also be encrypted at rest within the Kubernetes cluster.

- **Access Control**: Secrets are namespace-scoped and can be restricted to specific applications or users, minimizing the risk of unauthorized access.

- **Flexibility**: Like ConfigMaps, Secrets allow you to decouple sensitive configurations, making it easier to update them without modifying application code.

3. **Creating a Secret**:

- You can create a Secret from a YAML file or directly from the command line.

- **Example**: Creating a Secret for database credentials.

yaml
Copy code
apiVersion: v1
kind: Secret
metadata:

name: db-credentials

type: Opaque

data:

DB_USER: dXNlcm5hbWU=   # base64-encoded value of "username"

DB_PASSWORD: cGFzc3dvcmQ= # base64-encoded value of "password"

- o To base64-encode a string, you can use a command like:

bash
Copy code
echo -n 'username' | base64

- o Apply the Secret to the cluster:

bash
Copy code
kubectl apply -f db-credentials.yaml

4. **Using Secrets in Pods**:
   - o Similar to ConfigMaps, Secrets can be injected into containers as environment variables or mounted as files.
   - o **Example of using Secrets as environment variables** in a deployment:

```yaml
yaml
Copy code
apiVersion: apps/v1
kind: Deployment
metadata:
  name: app-deployment
spec:
  replicas: 1
  selector:
    matchLabels:
      app: myapp
  template:
    metadata:
      labels:
        app: myapp
    spec:
      containers:
      - name: app-container
        image: myapp:latest
        env:
        - name: DB_USER
          valueFrom:
            secretKeyRef:
              name: db-credentials
              key: DB_USER
```

```
- name: DB_PASSWORD
  valueFrom:
   secretKeyRef:
    name: db-credentials
    key: DB_PASSWORD
```

5. **Best Practices for Using Secrets**:
   o **Restrict Access**: Use Kubernetes' RBAC (Role-Based Access Control) to restrict access to Secrets based on application and user roles.
   o **Enable Encryption**: Enable Secret encryption at rest in the Kubernetes cluster to protect sensitive data from unauthorized access.
   o **Use Separate Namespaces**: For added security, keep sensitive secrets in separate namespaces to limit access and reduce risk.
   o **Avoid Plaintext Secrets**: Even though Secrets are base64-encoded, avoid storing them as plaintext files. Instead, use tools like HashiCorp Vault, AWS Secrets Manager, or GCP Secret Manager for added security.

Example Project: Creating a ConfigMap and a Secret for an Application's Environment Variables

Let's walk through a practical example of deploying a simple application with configurations stored in a ConfigMap and sensitive information managed as a Secret.

Step 1: Create the ConfigMap

1. **Define a ConfigMap** for a sample application, including configuration values like APP_ENV and LOG_LEVEL:

    yaml
    ```
    apiVersion: v1
    kind: ConfigMap
    metadata:
      name: app-config
    data:
      APP_ENV: "production"
      LOG_LEVEL: "info"
    ```

2. **Apply the ConfigMap** to the cluster:

    bash
    Copy code
    ```
    kubectl apply -f app-config.yaml
    ```

Step 2: Create the Secret

1. **Define a Secret** for database credentials:

yaml

Copy code

apiVersion: v1

kind: Secret

metadata:

  name: db-secret

type: Opaque

data:

  DB_USER: ZGJfdXNlcg==   # base64-encoded "db_user"

  DB_PASSWORD: c2VjdXJlcGFzcw==   #   base64-encoded "securepass"

2. **Apply the Secret** to the cluster:

bash

kubectl apply -f db-secret.yaml

Step 3: Create the Deployment

1. **Define the Deployment**:
   - o We'll use both the ConfigMap and the Secret as environment variables within the deployment.

     yaml

     Copy code

     apiVersion: apps/v1

```yaml
kind: Deployment
metadata:
  name: app-deployment
spec:
  replicas: 1
  selector:
    matchLabels:
      app: sample-app
  template:
    metadata:
      labels:
        app: sample-app
    spec:
      containers:
      - name: app-container
        image: sample-app:latest
        envFrom:
          - configMapRef:
              name: app-config
        env:
          - name: DB_USER
            valueFrom:
              secretKeyRef:
                name: db-secret
                key: DB_USER
```

```
- name: DB_PASSWORD
  valueFrom:
   secretKeyRef:
    name: db-secret
    key: DB_PASSWORD
```

2. **Deploy the Application**:
   o Save the deployment configuration as app-deployment.yaml and apply it:

   bash
   kubectl apply -f app-deployment.yaml

3. **Verify the Deployment**:
   o Check the status of the pods to ensure that the deployment is successful:

   bash
   Copy code
   kubectl get pods

Step 4: Verify Environment Variables

1. **Inspect Environment Variables**:
   o You can verify that the ConfigMap and Secret were loaded as environment variables by accessing the running container's environment:

bash

Copy code

kubectl exec -it <pod-name> -- env

- o Check for the variables APP_ENV, LOG_LEVEL, DB_USER, and DB_PASSWORD to confirm that both the ConfigMap and Secret were applied correctly.

In this chapter, we explored how to manage application configurations and sensitive data in Kubernetes using ConfigMaps and Secrets. We discussed the benefits of using ConfigMaps to decouple configurations from application code and highlighted best practices for securely managing sensitive data with Secrets. The example project demonstrated how to use both resources to configure a sample application, showing how to inject environment variables from ConfigMaps and Secrets into a deployment.

In the next chapter, we'll dive into **Kubernetes Volumes and Persistent Storage**, learning how to manage data that needs to persist beyond the lifecycle of individual pods.

CHAPTER 7: KUBERNETES VOLUMES AND PERSISTENT STORAGE

Data persistence is a critical aspect of managing applications, especially in Kubernetes, where containers and pods are designed to be ephemeral. In this chapter, we'll explore the difference between **ephemeral** and **persistent storage**, discuss various types of volumes in Kubernetes—particularly **Persistent Volumes (PV)** and **Persistent Volume Claims (PVC)**—and walk through a practical example of setting up persistent storage for a database application.

Ephemeral vs. Persistent Storage: Why Storage is Challenging in Kubernetes

1. **Ephemeral Storage**:
   - **Ephemeral** storage is temporary, meaning that data stored inside a pod or container is lost when the pod is restarted, rescheduled, or deleted.
   - This storage is ideal for applications that don't need data persistence, such as stateless web servers where any necessary data is either cached or stored externally.
   - **Challenge**: Stateless applications work well with ephemeral storage, but for applications like

databases, losing data on restart or failure can be detrimental.

2. **Persistent Storage**:

   o **Persistent storage** allows data to outlive the lifecycle of individual pods, which is essential for applications that rely on data durability, like databases, content management systems, and storage for user-generated content.

   o Persistent storage ensures that data is preserved even when pods are scaled, updated, or restarted.

   o **Why Storage is Challenging in Kubernetes**:

     ▪ Containers and pods are designed to be lightweight, disposable, and mobile. Kubernetes orchestrates pods to optimize availability and efficiency, which means that containers can move between nodes based on scheduling needs.

     ▪ Since data stored within a pod's container is lost when the pod is replaced or rescheduled, Kubernetes needs a way to provide storage that persists beyond the container's lifecycle and is accessible across nodes.

3. **The Solution: Kubernetes Volumes**:

   o Kubernetes uses **volumes** to provide data storage options for containers. Volumes are mounted within a pod and can persist even when containers within the pod are restarted.

- o **Persistent Volumes (PVs)** and **Persistent Volume Claims (PVCs)**, which we'll cover in detail, provide a mechanism for managing storage in Kubernetes that maintains data integrity across pod lifecycles.

Types of Volumes: Understanding Persistent Volumes (PV) and Persistent Volume Claims (PVC)

Kubernetes uses a combination of Persistent Volumes (PV) and Persistent Volume Claims (PVC) to manage persistent storage.

1. **Persistent Volumes (PVs)**:
    - o A **Persistent Volume** is a storage resource in a Kubernetes cluster, similar to a physical disk. PVs are created by administrators or dynamically provisioned and exist independently of any specific pod.
    - o PVs can be backed by a variety of storage providers, including **local disks**, **network file systems (NFS)**, and **cloud storage solutions** (e.g., AWS EBS, Google Persistent Disk).
    - o **Characteristics of PVs**:
        - PVs are cluster resources, not tied to any specific namespace or pod.

- They provide a fixed amount of storage and have a storage class and access mode.

  o **Creating a PV**:

  - The following YAML defines a PV of 1Gi capacity backed by NFS:

    ```yaml
    yaml
    apiVersion: v1
    kind: PersistentVolume
    metadata:
      name: example-pv
    spec:
      capacity:
        storage: 1Gi
      accessModes:
        - ReadWriteOnce
      persistentVolumeReclaimPolicy: Retain
      nfs:
        path: /path/to/storage
        server: nfs-server.example.com
    ```

  - **Access Modes**:

    - **ReadWriteOnce (RWO)**: The volume can be mounted as read-write by a single node.

- **ReadOnlyMany (ROX)**: The volume can be mounted as read-only by multiple nodes.
- **ReadWriteMany (RWX)**: The volume can be mounted as read-write by multiple nodes.

2. **Persistent Volume Claims (PVCs)**:
   - A **Persistent Volume Claim** is a request for storage by a pod. PVCs allow users to request specific storage resources, such as size and access mode, without knowing the details of the underlying storage.
   - PVCs are namespace-scoped, allowing developers to request storage for their applications in a way that's abstracted from the physical infrastructure.
   - **Characteristics of PVCs**:
     - PVCs dynamically bind to PVs that meet the requested criteria.
     - PVCs are used by pods to mount storage volumes, enabling persistent data storage across pod lifecycles.
   - **Creating a PVC**:
     - The following YAML defines a PVC requesting 500Mi of storage with ReadWriteOnce access:

```yaml
apiVersion: v1
kind: PersistentVolumeClaim
metadata:
 name: example-pvc
spec:
 accessModes:
  - ReadWriteOnce
 resources:
  requests:
   storage: 500Mi
```

- o When this PVC is created, Kubernetes attempts to bind it to an available PV that meets the request criteria. If no suitable PV exists, the PVC will wait until an appropriate PV becomes available.

3. **Storage Classes**:
   - o **Storage classes** define different types of storage based on performance, backup policy, or cost, which enables dynamic provisioning. For example, a storage class can define whether storage is backed by SSDs or HDDs, enabling applications to request storage based on performance needs.
   - o **Dynamic Provisioning**: Using storage classes, Kubernetes can automatically provision PVs to

satisfy PVCs, making storage management much easier.

Example: Setting Up Persistent Storage for a Database Application

Let's deploy a simple database (e.g., MySQL) and configure it to use persistent storage with a PV and PVC, ensuring data persists even if the database pod is restarted or rescheduled.

Step 1: Create a Persistent Volume (PV)

1. **Define a PV**:
   - The following YAML file defines a PV with 1Gi of storage and a ReadWriteOnce access mode, suitable for a database application.

   yaml
   apiVersion: v1
   kind: PersistentVolume
   metadata:
     name: mysql-pv
   spec:
     capacity:
       storage: 1Gi
     accessModes:
       - ReadWriteOnce
     persistentVolumeReclaimPolicy: Retain

```
        hostPath:
        path: /mnt/data/mysql
```

2. **Apply the PV**:
    o   Save this YAML as mysql-pv.yaml and apply it to
        the cluster:

```bash
kubectl apply -f mysql-pv.yaml
```

Step 2: Create a Persistent Volume Claim (PVC)

1. **Define a PVC**:
    o   The following YAML file defines a PVC that
        requests 1Gi of storage with a ReadWriteOnce
        access mode, matching the specifications of mysql-
        pv.

```yaml
apiVersion: v1
kind: PersistentVolumeClaim
metadata:
  name: mysql-pvc
spec:
  accessModes:
    - ReadWriteOnce
  resources:
```

requests:

storage: 1Gi

2. **Apply the PVC**:

   o Save this YAML as mysql-pvc.yaml and apply it:

   bash
   kubectl apply -f mysql-pvc.yaml

   o The PVC will automatically bind to mysql-pv if it matches the storage and access mode requirements.

Step 3: Deploy the MySQL Database Using the PVC

1. **Define the Deployment**:

   o The following YAML file defines a MySQL deployment, using the PVC as the storage for the MySQL data directory.

   yaml
   apiVersion: apps/v1
   kind: Deployment
   metadata:
     name: mysql
   spec:
     selector:
       matchLabels:

```yaml
    app: mysql
  replicas: 1
  template:
    metadata:
      labels:
        app: mysql
    spec:
      containers:
      - name: mysql
        image: mysql:5.7
        env:
          - name: MYSQL_ROOT_PASSWORD
            value: "password"
        volumeMounts:
          - mountPath: "/var/lib/mysql"
            name: mysql-storage
      volumes:
      - name: mysql-storage
        persistentVolumeClaim:
          claimName: mysql-pvc
```

- o **Explanation**:
  - **volumeMounts**: Mounts the PVC at /var/lib/mysql, where MySQL stores its data.
  - **volumes**: Defines the mysql-storage volume, linking it to the mysql-pvc.

2. **Apply the Deployment**:
    - o Save this YAML as mysql-deployment.yaml and apply it:

    bash

    Copy code

    kubectl apply -f mysql-deployment.yaml

Step 4: Verify the Persistent Storage

1. **Check the PVC and PV**:
    - o Ensure the PVC is bound to the PV by running:

    bash

    kubectl get pvc

    - o Check the PV's status:

    bash

    kubectl get pv

2. **Test Data Persistence**:
    - o Access the MySQL pod and create a sample database:

    bash

    kubectl exec -it <mysql-pod-name> -- mysql -u root -p

CREATE DATABASE test_db;

- o Delete the MySQL pod:

  bash
  kubectl delete pod <mysql-pod-name>

- o When the pod restarts, reconnect to the MySQL instance and verify that test_db still exists, demonstrating data persistence.

In this chapter, we explored how Kubernetes manages storage using **volumes**, particularly **Persistent Volumes (PV)** and **Persistent Volume Claims (PVC)**, to ensure data persists across pod lifecycles. We discussed the differences between ephemeral and persistent storage, why persistent storage is essential for stateful applications, and walked through a practical example of setting up persistent storage for a MySQL database.

In the next chapter, we'll explore **Stateful Applications on Kubernetes** in more detail, learning about StatefulSets and how Kubernetes manages stateful workloads.

CHAPTER 8: STATEFUL APPLICATIONS ON KUBERNETES

While Kubernetes is naturally suited for managing stateless applications, many applications require persistent state and continuity across pod lifecycles, such as databases and caching systems. In this chapter, we'll cover the key differences between **stateless** and **stateful applications**, introduce **StatefulSets**—the Kubernetes resource designed to handle stateful applications—and walk through a real-world example of deploying a stateful application like Redis.

Difference Between Stateless and Stateful Applications: Use Cases for Each

1. **Stateless Applications**:
   - **Definition**: Stateless applications don't retain data or state between requests. Each interaction with the application is independent of previous ones, so if a stateless application is restarted, it doesn't need to retain any information about prior interactions.
   - **Characteristics**:
     - Can be scaled easily, as instances don't rely on previous states.

- Often more resilient to failures, as individual instances can be replaced or restarted without affecting data integrity.
- Easier to distribute across multiple nodes and regions.

o **Examples**:
- Web servers, front-end services, and microservices that process data but don't need to save it (e.g., load balancers, content servers, API gateways).

2. **Stateful Applications**:

o **Definition**: Stateful applications retain data or state across sessions or requests, meaning they need to remember previous interactions and maintain data continuity even if the application is restarted or scaled.

o **Characteristics**:
- Scaling is more complex, as each instance might need to retain unique data.
- Stateful applications typically require persistent storage to save data across restarts.
- They may need specific identity or ordering to ensure proper data handling and recovery.

o **Examples**:

- Databases, messaging systems (like Kafka), distributed caches (like Redis), and applications with session data.

3. **Choosing Between Stateless and Stateful Approaches**:
   - For simple, scalable workloads that don't require persistence, stateless applications are ideal.
   - For applications that handle data storage, transactions, or need session consistency, stateful applications are necessary, and Kubernetes provides StatefulSets to handle their specific requirements.

Working with StatefulSets: How Kubernetes Handles Stateful Applications

What is a StatefulSet?

- A **StatefulSet** is a Kubernetes resource designed specifically for managing stateful applications. Unlike Deployments, which treat each pod as identical and interchangeable, StatefulSets maintain pod identity and ordering.
- StatefulSets ensure that each pod has a stable, unique identifier, enabling Kubernetes to manage stateful applications where persistence and order are crucial.

Key Features of StatefulSets:

1. **Stable, Unique Network Identity**:

- o Each pod in a StatefulSet has a unique hostname based on its ordinal index (e.g., pod-0, pod-1). This hostname remains the same even if the pod is restarted, making it easier to maintain connections.
- o For example, if you have a StatefulSet named redis, the pods will be named redis-0, redis-1, etc.

2. **Stable Storage**:
   - o StatefulSets can associate each pod with a Persistent Volume (PV), ensuring that data remains intact across pod restarts. Each pod has its own dedicated PV, so data from redis-0 will not mix with redis-1.
   - o Persistent Volume Claims (PVCs) are used to dynamically provision storage for each pod in the StatefulSet.

3. **Ordered Deployment and Scaling**:
   - o StatefulSets deploy, scale, and delete pods in a specific order. For example, pod redis-0 will be created before redis-1, and deletion will occur in the reverse order.
   - o This ordered approach ensures that dependencies are met, which is particularly useful for databases or distributed systems where initialization order matters.

4. **Use Cases for StatefulSets**:

- o **Databases**: Relational and NoSQL databases (e.g., MySQL, Cassandra) that need persistent storage.
- o **Distributed Caches**: Systems like Redis that require data consistency and stable connections.
- o **Message Queues**: Kafka clusters where data partitions are distributed across nodes.

Real-World Example: Deploying a Stateful Application Like Redis

Let's deploy Redis using a StatefulSet in Kubernetes to see how StatefulSets work with a real-world, stateful application. Redis is an in-memory data structure store commonly used as a database, cache, and message broker.

Step 1: Create a Persistent Volume Claim Template

1. **Define a PVC Template**:
   - o StatefulSets require a template for the PVCs to create storage for each Redis pod. Here's an example YAML file defining the PVC template for Redis:

     yaml
     apiVersion: v1
     kind: PersistentVolumeClaim
     metadata:
       name: redis-storage

```
spec:
  accessModes:
    - ReadWriteOnce
  resources:
    requests:
      storage: 1Gi
```

2. **Save and Apply the PVC Template**:
   - Save this file as redis-pvc.yaml and apply it:

   bash
   kubectl apply -f redis-pvc.yaml

Step 2: Create the Redis StatefulSet

1. **Define the StatefulSet**:
   - The following YAML file defines a StatefulSet with two Redis replicas, each using its own persistent storage. The Redis StatefulSet will ensure each pod has a unique identity and its own storage volume.

   yaml
   ```
   apiVersion: apps/v1
   kind: StatefulSet
   metadata:
     name: redis
   spec:
   ```

```
serviceName: "redis"
replicas: 2
selector:
 matchLabels:
  app: redis
template:
 metadata:
  labels:
   app: redis
 spec:
  containers:
  - name: redis
    image: redis:6.0
    ports:
    - containerPort: 6379
    volumeMounts:
    - name: redis-storage
      mountPath: /data
volumeClaimTemplates:
- metadata:
   name: redis-storage
  spec:
   accessModes: [ "ReadWriteOnce" ]
   resources:
    requests:
```

storage: 1Gi

- o **Explanation**:
  - **serviceName**: A headless service named redis allows each pod in the StatefulSet to be accessed via a unique network identity.
  - **replicas**: The StatefulSet will create two Redis replicas (redis-0 and redis-1), each with its own identity.
  - **volumeClaimTemplates**: Each pod will get its own PVC named redis-storage, allowing persistent storage for each Redis instance.

2. **Deploy the StatefulSet**:
   - o Save this YAML as redis-statefulset.yaml and apply it:

   bash
   kubectl apply -f redis-statefulset.yaml

3. **Check the Status of the StatefulSet**:
   - o Verify that the StatefulSet is running and each Redis pod has been created:

   kubectl get statefulset

   - o You should see two Redis pods named redis-0 and redis-1.

1. **Create a Headless Service**:

   o To allow applications within the cluster to communicate with Redis, create a headless service. This service provides a stable network identity for each Redis pod.

   ```yaml
   yaml
   apiVersion: v1
   kind: Service
   metadata:
     name: redis
   spec:
     clusterIP: None
     selector:
       app: redis
     ports:
     - port: 6379
   ```

2. **Apply the Service**:

   o Save this as redis-service.yaml and apply it:

   ```bash
   bash
   kubectl apply -f redis-service.yaml
   ```

   o **Explanation**:

- By setting clusterIP: None, the service becomes a headless service. This allows each Redis pod in the StatefulSet to be accessed individually by hostname (e.g., redis-0.redis, redis-1.redis).

Step 4: Verify the Deployment and Test Redis

1. **Verify the Pods**:
   - Check that each Redis pod has been assigned its unique identity:

   bash
   kubectl get pods -l app=redis

2. **Access Redis**:
   - Access one of the Redis instances (e.g., redis-0) to test its functionality:

   bash
   Copy code
   kubectl exec -it redis-0 -- redis-cli

   - In the Redis CLI, you can test data persistence by setting a key-value pair:

   bash

```
Copy code
set mykey "Hello, Kubernetes"
get mykey
```

3. **Test Data Persistence**:
   o To confirm persistence, delete the redis-0 pod:

   ```bash
   Copy code
   kubectl delete pod redis-0
   ```

   o Kubernetes will automatically recreate redis-0, preserving its unique identity and PVC. After it restarts, connect to it again and check if mykey still exists:

   ```bash
   get mykey
   ```

   o If the data is still present, this confirms that the PVC is functioning correctly, preserving data across pod restarts.

In this chapter, we explored the differences between **stateless** and **stateful applications** and introduced **StatefulSets**, which Kubernetes provides to manage applications requiring persistent storage and stable identity. We also walked through a real-world example of deploying Redis as a StatefulSet, configuring persistent storage for each Redis instance, and verifying data persistence. By using StatefulSets, Kubernetes enables complex applications, like databases and caching systems, to maintain state across pod lifecycles, providing reliability and continuity in distributed environments.

In the next chapter, we'll dive into **Ingress and Traffic Management**, where we'll learn how to manage and control external access to services in a Kubernetes cluster.

CHAPTER 9: INGRESS AND TRAFFIC MANAGEMENT

Managing external access to services is an essential part of deploying applications in Kubernetes. **Ingress** is the Kubernetes resource that enables traffic management by providing a unified way to control external access to multiple services within a cluster. In this chapter, we'll explore **Ingress Controllers**, learn how to set up **Ingress Rules** for routing traffic to different applications, and walk through an example project of configuring an Ingress resource for a web application with multiple routes.

Understanding Ingress Controllers: How Kubernetes Handles Incoming Traffic

1. **What is an Ingress?**

   o An **Ingress** is a Kubernetes resource that manages external access to services within a cluster, typically HTTP and HTTPS traffic. It provides a way to define rules for routing requests to different services based on paths or domains.

   o Ingress consolidates multiple services under a single endpoint (such as example.com), allowing you to route traffic to different applications based on URI paths or subdomains.

2. **The Role of an Ingress Controller**:

- o While an Ingress defines the routing rules, an **Ingress Controller** is responsible for interpreting those rules and actually routing the traffic accordingly.
- o Kubernetes doesn't include an Ingress Controller by default, so you need to install one. Popular Ingress Controllers include **NGINX Ingress Controller**, **Traefik**, and **HAProxy**.
- o **How Ingress Controllers Work**:
  - The Ingress Controller monitors the cluster for new Ingress resources.
  - It configures the appropriate routes and load-balancing rules based on the Ingress definitions.
  - When external requests arrive, the Ingress Controller routes them to the appropriate services, applying load balancing, SSL termination, and other configurations as needed.

3. **Benefits of Using Ingress**:
   - o **Simplified Management**: Ingress allows you to expose multiple services through a single IP address, simplifying DNS and networking configurations.

- o **Traffic Control**: Provides centralized control over routing, including support for path-based routing, host-based routing, and SSL/TLS termination.
- o **Enhanced Security**: Ingress Controllers offer features like HTTPS support, rate limiting, and custom authentication mechanisms, enhancing the security of exposed services.

Setting Up Ingress Rules: Routing External Traffic to Applications

1. **Defining Ingress Rules**:
   - o Ingress rules specify how traffic should be routed based on the host or path of incoming requests.
   - o **Host-Based Routing**: Routes traffic based on the requested hostname, allowing multiple applications to be accessible through subdomains (e.g., app1.example.com, app2.example.com).
   - o **Path-Based Routing**: Routes traffic based on the URL path, so different services are accessible on the same hostname but with different paths (e.g., example.com/app1, example.com/app2).

2. **Configuring Basic Ingress Rules**:
   - o Here's a basic Ingress configuration for routing traffic to two different services (app1 and app2) based on URL paths:

```yaml
apiVersion: networking.k8s.io/v1
kind: Ingress
metadata:
  name: example-ingress
  annotations:
    nginx.ingress.kubernetes.io/rewrite-target: /
spec:
  rules:
  - host: "example.com"
    http:
      paths:
      - path: /app1
        pathType: Prefix
        backend:
          service:
            name: app1-service
            port:
              number: 80
      - path: /app2
        pathType: Prefix
        backend:
          service:
            name: app2-service
            port:
```

number: 80

- o **Explanation**:
    - The host field specifies the domain name (example.com), while each path defines a rule for routing traffic to different backend services (app1-service and app2-service) based on the URL path.

3. **Annotations for Advanced Configuration**:
   - o Ingress Controllers use **annotations** to configure additional features, such as SSL termination, URL rewrites, and custom error pages.
   - o Example annotations for HTTPS and URL rewrites:
       - nginx.ingress.kubernetes.io/rewrite-target: /: Rewrites the URL to match the backend service.
       - nginx.ingress.kubernetes.io/ssl-redirect: "true": Redirects HTTP requests to HTTPS.

4. **TLS Configuration for HTTPS**:
   - o To serve traffic over HTTPS, you need to configure TLS in your Ingress. This involves creating a **Kubernetes Secret** containing the SSL certificate and key.
   - o Example:
       - First, create the TLS secret:

bash

```
kubectl create secret tls example-tls --
cert=path/to/tls.crt --key=path/to/tls.key
```

- Update the Ingress to reference the TLS secret:

yaml

```
spec:
 tls:
 - hosts:
   - example.com
   secretName: example-tls
```

Example Project: Configuring an Ingress Resource for a Web Application with Multiple Routes

In this example, we'll deploy two simple applications, app1 and app2, and configure an Ingress resource to route external traffic to each application based on the URL path.

Step 1: Deploy the Applications

1. **Create Deployments and Services for app1 and app2**:
   o Here's a sample YAML for deploying app1:

   yaml
   ```
   apiVersion: apps/v1
   kind: Deployment
   ```

```
metadata:
 name: app1
spec:
 replicas: 1
 selector:
  matchLabels:
   app: app1
 template:
  metadata:
   labels:
    app: app1
  spec:
   containers:
   - name: app1
     image: nginx
     ports:
     - containerPort: 80
```

- o Create a similar deployment for app2 by replacing app1 with app2.

2. **Create Services for app1 and app2**:
   - o Define ClusterIP services for each application to expose them internally within the cluster.

```
yaml
apiVersion: v1
```

```
kind: Service
metadata:
  name: app1-service
spec:
  selector:
    app: app1
  ports:
  - protocol: TCP
    port: 80
    targetPort: 80
```

  o Create a similar service for app2.

3. **Apply the Deployments and Services**:
  o Save each file and apply them to the cluster:

```bash
kubectl apply -f app1-deployment.yaml
kubectl apply -f app1-service.yaml
kubectl apply -f app2-deployment.yaml
kubectl apply -f app2-service.yaml
```

Step 2: Install an Ingress Controller

1. **Install the NGINX Ingress Controller** (if it's not already installed):
  o Use the following command to install the NGINX Ingress Controller with kubectl:

bash

kubectl apply -f https://raw.githubusercontent.com/kubernetes/ingres s- nginx/main/deploy/static/provider/cloud/deploy.ya ml

o   Verify that the Ingress Controller pods are running:

bash

kubectl get pods -n ingress-nginx

Step 3: Create the Ingress Resource

1. **Define the Ingress Resource**:

   o   Here's a YAML file for an Ingress resource that routes traffic to app1 and app2 based on the URL path.

yaml
apiVersion: networking.k8s.io/v1
kind: Ingress
metadata:
  name: app-ingress
  annotations:
    nginx.ingress.kubernetes.io/rewrite-target: /
spec:

```
rules:
- host: "example.com"
  http:
    paths:
    - path: /app1
      pathType: Prefix
      backend:
        service:
          name: app1-service
          port:
            number: 80
    - path: /app2
      pathType: Prefix
      backend:
        service:
          name: app2-service
          port:
            number: 80
```

2. **Apply the Ingress Resource**:
   o Save this file as app-ingress.yaml and apply it:

   bash

   kubectl apply -f app-ingress.yaml

Step 4: Test the Ingress Setup

1. **Edit Your Hosts File (Local Testing Only)**:
   - ○ Since example.com is a placeholder, you'll need to map it to your Ingress Controller's external IP for testing.
   - ○ Get the external IP of the Ingress Controller:

   bash
   ```
   kubectl get services -o wide -w -n ingress-nginx
   ```

   - ○ Edit your /etc/hosts file (or C:\Windows\System32\drivers\etc\hosts on Windows) to map example.com to the external IP:

   kotlin
   ```
   <external-ip> example.com
   ```

2. **Access the Applications**:
   - ○ Open a browser and test the following URLs:
     - ▪ http://example.com/app1: You should see the default nginx page served by app1.
     - ▪ http://example.com/app2: You should see the default nginx page served by app2.
   - ○ Kubernetes routes the traffic based on the paths defined in the Ingress resource.

In this chapter, we explored **Ingress** in Kubernetes, a powerful resource for managing external access and traffic routing. We discussed **Ingress Controllers**, which interpret Ingress resources and handle the routing of external traffic to the appropriate services within the cluster. We also covered **Ingress rules** for path-based and host-based routing and walked through a practical example of deploying two applications and routing traffic to each based on URL paths.

In the next chapter, we'll dive into **Kubernetes Resource Management**, where we'll learn how to control and optimize the allocation of resources like CPU and memory across applications.

CHAPTER 10: KUBERNETES RESOURCE MANAGEMENT

Efficient resource management is critical for ensuring that applications run smoothly without consuming excessive resources or impacting other workloads. In Kubernetes, **Resource Requests** and **Limits** help manage CPU and memory allocation, while **Namespaces** provide a way to organize and isolate resources for different applications or teams. This chapter covers these concepts in detail, showing how they contribute to efficient and reliable application deployments. We'll also walk through an example of setting resource limits for applications in production and testing environments.

Resource Requests and Limits: Managing CPU and Memory Allocations

1. **Understanding Resource Requests**:
   - A **Resource Request** specifies the minimum amount of CPU and memory that a container requires to run effectively. Kubernetes uses these requests to determine where to schedule the pod, ensuring the container receives enough resources.
   - **CPU and Memory Units**:
     - **CPU**: Measured in CPU units. 1 CPU in Kubernetes is equivalent to 1 vCPU on cloud providers or 1 physical core in a bare-metal machine. You can also specify

fractional CPU requests (e.g., 500m for 0.5 CPU).

- **Memory**: Measured in bytes, commonly specified in Mi (Mebibytes) or Gi (Gibibytes).

o **Example**:

```yaml
resources:
  requests:
    cpu: "250m"   # Minimum 0.25 CPU
    memory: "128Mi"   # Minimum 128 MiB memory
```

2. **Understanding Resource Limits**:

o A **Resource Limit** defines the maximum amount of CPU and memory that a container can consume. If a container exceeds its limit, Kubernetes may throttle its CPU usage or terminate the container if it exceeds the memory limit.

o Resource limits help prevent "noisy neighbor" issues, where one application consumes excessive resources, affecting other applications.

o **Example**:

```yaml
```

```
Copy code
resources:
  limits:
    cpu: "500m"    # Maximum 0.5 CPU
    memory: "256Mi"    # Maximum 256 MiB
memory
```

3. **Best Practices for Setting Resource Requests and Limits**:
   - ○ **Balance Requests and Limits**: Set realistic resource requests and limits based on application requirements. Too low, and the app may fail under load; too high, and it may limit resources for other applications.
   - ○ **Monitor Usage Patterns**: Use monitoring tools like **Prometheus** and **Grafana** to understand the resource usage patterns of your applications, which can guide you in setting appropriate values.
   - ○ **Adjust for Environment**: Set different resource limits for development, testing, and production environments based on the load and criticality of the application.

4. **Example Resource Configuration**:
   - ○ Here's a YAML configuration for a container with both requests and limits set:

   yaml

```
Copy code
apiVersion: v1
kind: Pod
metadata:
  name: example-pod
spec:
  containers:
  - name: example-container
    image: nginx
    resources:
      requests:
        cpu: "250m"
        memory: "128Mi"
      limits:
        cpu: "500m"
        memory: "256Mi"
```

o In this configuration, the container requests a minimum of 0.25 CPU and 128 MiB of memory and is limited to a maximum of 0.5 CPU and 256 MiB of memory.

Namespaces for Resource Isolation: Organizing Applications and Environments

1. **What are Namespaces?**

o **Namespaces** in Kubernetes are virtual clusters within a physical cluster. They help organize and isolate resources, allowing multiple teams, applications, or environments to coexist within the same cluster without interfering with one another.

o Namespaces are useful for managing multi-tenant environments, separating development, testing, and production environments, and providing resource isolation for different teams.

2. **Creating and Using Namespaces**:

o To create a namespace, you can use the following YAML file:

```yaml
apiVersion: v1
kind: Namespace
metadata:
  name: dev-environment
```

o Apply the namespace:

```bash
kubectl apply -f dev-namespace.yaml
```

3. **Assigning Resources to Namespaces**:

- o When deploying resources, you can specify a namespace using the -n flag in kubectl or by defining it in the YAML metadata:

```yaml
metadata:
  name: app-deployment
  namespace: dev-environment
```

- o You can also switch your kubectl context to a specific namespace:

```bash
kubectl config set-context --current --namespace=dev-environment
```

4. **Resource Quotas for Namespaces**:
   - o Kubernetes allows you to set **ResourceQuotas** within namespaces to control the total CPU, memory, and other resources allocated to that namespace. This helps ensure that no single team or application consumes excessive resources.
   - o **Example Resource Quota**:

```yaml
apiVersion: v1
kind: ResourceQuota
```

```
metadata:
  name: dev-quota
  namespace: dev-environment
spec:
  hard:
    requests.cpu: "2"
    requests.memory: "4Gi"
    limits.cpu: "4"
    limits.memory: "8Gi"
```

- o In this example, the dev-environment namespace is limited to 2 CPU requests, 4 CPU limits, 4 GiB of memory requests, and 8 GiB of memory limits.

Example Scenario: Configuring Resource Limits for Applications in Production and Testing Environments

In this example, we'll configure resource requests and limits for a web application in both production and testing environments, using namespaces and ResourceQuotas to ensure resource isolation.

Step 1: Set Up Namespaces for Production and Testing

1. **Create the Production and Testing Namespaces**:
   - o Define namespaces for production and testing:

   yaml
   apiVersion: v1

```
kind: Namespace
metadata:
  name: production
---
apiVersion: v1
kind: Namespace
metadata:
  name: testing
```

- o Apply these configurations:

```bash
kubectl apply -f namespaces.yaml
```

Step 2: Define ResourceQuotas for Each Namespace

1. **Create ResourceQuotas for Production**:
   - o Set generous ResourceQuotas for production to handle high traffic and demanding workloads:

```yaml
apiVersion: v1
kind: ResourceQuota
metadata:
  name: production-quota
  namespace: production
spec:
```

```
hard:
  requests.cpu: "10"
  requests.memory: "20Gi"
  limits.cpu: "20"
  limits.memory: "40Gi"
```

○ Save as production-quota.yaml and apply it:

```bash
kubectl apply -f production-quota.yaml
```

2. **Create ResourceQuotas for Testing**:

   ○ Set more restrictive ResourceQuotas for testing, where applications typically require fewer resources:

```yaml
apiVersion: v1
kind: ResourceQuota
metadata:
  name: testing-quota
  namespace: testing
spec:
  hard:
    requests.cpu: "2"
    requests.memory: "4Gi"
    limits.cpu: "4"
    limits.memory: "8Gi"
```

> o   Save as testing-quota.yaml and apply it:

```bash
Copy code
kubectl apply -f testing-quota.yaml
```

Step 3: Configure Resource Requests and Limits in the Application Deployments

1. **Define the Production Deployment**:
    - o   Here's an example production deployment configuration with resource requests and limits to ensure high availability and performance.

```yaml
apiVersion: apps/v1
kind: Deployment
metadata:
  name: web-app
  namespace: production
spec:
  replicas: 3
  selector:
    matchLabels:
      app: web-app
  template:
    metadata:
```

```
    labels:
      app: web-app
   spec:
    containers:
    - name: web-app-container
      image: nginx
      resources:
        requests:
          cpu: "500m"
          memory: "512Mi"
        limits:
          cpu: "1"
          memory: "1Gi"
```

○ Apply this deployment:

bash
kubectl apply -f production-deployment.yaml

2. **Define the Testing Deployment**:

○ For testing, we'll set lower requests and limits to avoid resource contention, as these environments generally don't need the same capacity.

yaml
Copy code
apiVersion: apps/v1

```
kind: Deployment
metadata:
  name: web-app
  namespace: testing
spec:
  replicas: 1
  selector:
    matchLabels:
      app: web-app
  template:
    metadata:
      labels:
        app: web-app
    spec:
      containers:
      - name: web-app-container
        image: nginx
        resources:
          requests:
            cpu: "100m"
            memory: "128Mi"
          limits:
            cpu: "200m"
            memory: "256Mi"
```

o   Apply this deployment:

bash

kubectl apply -f testing-deployment.yaml

Step 4: Verify Resource Allocation and Isolation

1. **Check the ResourceQuotas**:
   - View ResourceQuotas for production and testing:

   bash
   kubectl get resourcequota -n production
   kubectl get resourcequota -n testing

2. **Monitor Resource Usage**:
   - Use Kubernetes monitoring tools or kubectl to verify that resource usage remains within the allocated quotas, ensuring that production and testing environments don't impact each other.

In this chapter, we explored Kubernetes resource management, focusing on **Resource Requests** and **Limits** for CPU and memory to ensure optimal allocation. We discussed **Namespaces** as a way to organize and isolate resources for different environments, and we learned how to apply **ResourceQuotas** within namespaces to prevent any single environment from overusing resources. Finally, we walked through an example scenario where resource requests and limits were configured for a web application deployed in both production and testing environments, demonstrating how Kubernetes ensures efficient resource usage and isolation

CHAPTER 11: AUTOSCALING AND LOAD MANAGEMENT

Autoscaling is a key feature in Kubernetes that helps ensure applications and clusters can handle fluctuating traffic and workload demands. Kubernetes provides tools like the **Horizontal Pod Autoscaler** (HPA) to scale applications based on resource utilization and **Cluster Autoscaler** to dynamically adjust the number of nodes in a cluster. In this chapter, we'll dive into both types of autoscaling and walk through an example of using HPA to autoscale a high-traffic application based on real-world metrics.

Horizontal Pod Autoscaler: Scaling Applications Based on Resource Utilization

1. **What is the Horizontal Pod Autoscaler (HPA)?**
   - The **Horizontal Pod Autoscaler** (HPA) automatically adjusts the number of pod replicas for a deployment, replication controller, or stateful application based on CPU, memory, or custom metrics.
   - HPA continuously monitors the resource usage of an application and scales up or down based on the defined target thresholds, helping applications handle traffic spikes and maintain performance.

2. **How HPA Works**:

o The HPA checks the resource utilization metrics of each pod and compares them to a defined target (e.g., keeping CPU usage at or below 50%).

o If resource usage exceeds the target, HPA increases the number of replicas. If resource usage falls below the target, HPA decreases the replicas.

o HPA relies on Kubernetes metrics, which can be gathered from the **Metrics Server** or other monitoring tools like Prometheus.

3. **Setting Up the Horizontal Pod Autoscaler**:

o First, ensure that the **Metrics Server** is running in the cluster. The Metrics Server collects resource usage data that HPA uses to make scaling decisions.

bash

```
kubectl apply -f https://github.com/kubernetes-sigs/metrics-server/releases/latest/download/components.yaml
```

4. **Example HPA Configuration**:

o Here's an example of configuring HPA to autoscale a web application based on CPU usage:

yaml

```
apiVersion: autoscaling/v2
kind: HorizontalPodAutoscaler
```

```
metadata:
 name: web-app-hpa
 namespace: production
spec:
 scaleTargetRef:
  apiVersion: apps/v1
  kind: Deployment
  name: web-app
 minReplicas: 2
 maxReplicas: 10
 metrics:
 - type: Resource
  resource:
   name: cpu
   target:
    type: Utilization
    averageUtilization: 50
```

- o **Explanation**:
  - ▪ scaleTargetRef: Specifies the deployment (in this case, web-app) that the HPA will manage.
  - ▪ minReplicas and maxReplicas: Define the minimum and maximum number of pod replicas.

- metrics: Sets the scaling criteria—in this example, HPA will attempt to keep CPU usage at or below 50% by adjusting the number of replicas.

5. **Custom Metrics for Autoscaling**:
    - Besides CPU and memory, you can configure HPA to use custom metrics (e.g., request count, latency) if you have an external monitoring setup like Prometheus.
    - Custom metrics allow for more fine-tuned scaling based on specific application needs, such as API response time or queue length.

Cluster Autoscaling: Expanding the Cluster to Handle Increased Load

1. **What is the Cluster Autoscaler?**
    - The **Cluster Autoscaler** adjusts the number of nodes in a Kubernetes cluster based on the workloads' needs. When the HPA scales up an application and additional nodes are needed to accommodate the new pods, the Cluster Autoscaler adds nodes to the cluster.
    - Conversely, if node usage drops, the Cluster Autoscaler can remove underutilized nodes to reduce costs.

2. **How Cluster Autoscaler Works**:

   o The Cluster Autoscaler monitors pending pods that cannot be scheduled due to insufficient resources. It then adjusts the number of nodes in the cluster to meet the demand.

   o Once workloads decrease, the Cluster Autoscaler can also identify and remove underutilized nodes to optimize resource usage.

3. **Setting Up Cluster Autoscaler**:

   o Cluster Autoscaler is typically configured when deploying Kubernetes on cloud providers like AWS, GCP, and Azure. These providers offer managed Cluster Autoscalers that integrate directly with the cloud infrastructure.

   o **Example on Google Kubernetes Engine (GKE)**:

   bash
   ```
   gcloud container clusters update my-cluster \
     --enable-autoscaling \
     --min-nodes=1 \
     --max-nodes=10 \
     --zone us-central1-a
   ```

   o This command configures Cluster Autoscaler for a cluster with a minimum of 1 node and a maximum of 10 nodes, allowing it to scale based on demand.

4. **Benefits of Using Cluster Autoscaler**:

   o **Cost-Effective Scaling**: Automatically adjusts resources based on demand, which reduces costs during low-demand periods.

   o **Optimal Performance**: Ensures that applications have enough resources, even during traffic spikes, by adding nodes to the cluster when necessary.

   o **Efficient Resource Utilization**: Removes idle nodes, helping to avoid wasted resources and keeping the cluster lean.

Example: Autoscaling a High-Traffic Application with Real-World Metrics

Let's set up autoscaling for a web application deployment using HPA and test it with CPU load to observe how Kubernetes scales the application in response to increased traffic.

Step 1: Deploy a Sample Web Application

1. **Create the Deployment**:

   o Define a basic deployment for a sample web application (using nginx in this example) with resource requests and limits to trigger autoscaling:

   yaml
   Copy code
   apiVersion: apps/v1

```yaml
kind: Deployment
metadata:
  name: web-app
  namespace: production
spec:
  replicas: 2
  selector:
    matchLabels:
      app: web-app
  template:
    metadata:
      labels:
        app: web-app
    spec:
      containers:
      - name: nginx
        image: nginx
        resources:
          requests:
            cpu: "100m"
            memory: "128Mi"
          limits:
            cpu: "200m"
            memory: "256Mi"
        ports:
```

            - containerPort: 80

2. **Apply the Deployment**:
   o Save this file as web-app-deployment.yaml and deploy it to the production namespace:

   bash
   kubectl apply -f web-app-deployment.yaml

Step 2: Configure Horizontal Pod Autoscaler for the Web Application

1. **Set Up the HPA**:
   o Define an HPA that scales the web-app deployment based on CPU usage, aiming to keep CPU utilization at 50%:

   yaml
   apiVersion: autoscaling/v2
   kind: HorizontalPodAutoscaler
   metadata:
     name: web-app-hpa
     namespace: production
   spec:
     scaleTargetRef:
       apiVersion: apps/v1
       kind: Deployment

```
name: web-app
minReplicas: 2
maxReplicas: 10
metrics:
- type: Resource
  resource:
    name: cpu
    target:
      type: Utilization
      averageUtilization: 50
```

2. **Apply the HPA Configuration**:
   - Save this file as web-app-hpa.yaml and apply it:

   bash
   kubectl apply -f web-app-hpa.yaml

3. **Verify HPA Setup**:
   - Check the HPA status to confirm it's monitoring the web-app deployment:

   bash
   kubectl get hpa -n production

Step 3: Simulate High Traffic to Trigger Autoscaling

1. **Generate Load**:

o Use a load-testing tool like kubectl exec with a loop command or an external tool (e.g., Apache Benchmark or hey) to simulate high traffic:

bash
```
kubectl run -i --tty load-generator --image=busybox
--restart=Never -- /bin/sh -c "while true; do wget -q
-O- http://web-app.production.svc.cluster.local;
done"
```

2. **Monitor HPA Scaling**:
   o Watch the HPA status and the number of pod replicas to see if scaling occurs:

bash
Copy code
```
kubectl get hpa -n production
kubectl get pods -n production -l app=web-app -w
```

3. **Observe Autoscaling Behavior**:
   o As CPU usage increases, HPA should scale up the web-app deployment to meet demand by creating additional replicas.
   o When traffic decreases, HPA will reduce the number of replicas back down to the minimum to optimize resource usage.

Step 4: Configure Cluster Autoscaler (Optional)

1. **Set Up Cluster Autoscaler**:
   - If running on a managed Kubernetes platform, configure the Cluster Autoscaler with a minimum and maximum node count.
   - The Cluster Autoscaler will add nodes if HPA scales up the application to a point where existing nodes can no longer meet the demand.

2. **Test Cluster Autoscaling**:
   - Continue monitoring the cluster to ensure that when HPA increases the number of replicas, the Cluster Autoscaler adds nodes to support additional pods if necessary.

In this chapter, we explored autoscaling in Kubernetes, focusing on **Horizontal Pod Autoscaler** for scaling applications based on resource utilization and **Cluster Autoscaler** for adjusting the number of nodes in the cluster. We walked through configuring HPA to autoscale a web application based on CPU metrics and saw how to simulate high traffic to observe autoscaling in action. Kubernetes autoscaling provides a powerful and flexible way to handle dynamic workloads, optimize resource usage, and control costs.

In the next chapter, we'll cover **Monitoring and Logging in Kubernetes**, which will include setting up tools like Prometheus and Grafana to observe metrics, logs, and events within the cluster.

CHAPTER 12: MONITORING AND LOGGING IN KUBERNETES

Effective monitoring and logging are essential in Kubernetes to ensure applications are performing well and to quickly diagnose any issues. Kubernetes observability combines metrics, logs, and event monitoring to give a complete view of system health. In this chapter, we'll introduce **Kubernetes observability**, cover how to set up **Prometheus and Grafana** for monitoring, and walk through a practical example of configuring these tools to monitor a sample application.

Introduction to Kubernetes Observability: What to Monitor and Why

1. **What is Observability in Kubernetes?**
   - **Observability** refers to the ability to gain insight into the internal state of a system through monitoring and logging. It involves tracking metrics, logs, and events to understand system behavior, detect issues, and troubleshoot problems effectively.
   - In Kubernetes, observability is especially important due to the complex, dynamic nature of containerized environments.
2. **Key Components to Monitor in Kubernetes**:
   - **Cluster Health**:

- Monitor overall cluster status, including node availability, resource utilization (CPU, memory), and pod status.
- Issues like node failures, resource contention, or pod crashes can affect application availability.

o **Application Performance**:
- Track application metrics such as request latency, response times, error rates, and traffic volume to ensure reliable user experience.

o **Pod and Container Health**:
- Monitor pod status, restarts, CPU/memory usage, and error rates. This data helps identify issues like resource constraints, crashes, or OOM (out-of-memory) events.

o **Networking**:
- Observe network traffic, ingress/egress rates, and connectivity between services to detect network bottlenecks or configuration issues.

o **Resource Utilization**:
- Track CPU and memory usage across namespaces, nodes, and applications. This data is vital for making decisions around scaling and resource allocation.

- o **Event Logs**:
  - Collect logs of events like pod creation, deletion, and error messages to help identify trends, configuration issues, or security events.

3. **Why Observability is Important**:
   - o **Preventing Downtime**: Continuous monitoring of critical metrics helps detect anomalies early, preventing unexpected downtime.
   - o **Optimizing Resource Usage**: By tracking usage patterns, you can optimize resource allocation and avoid unnecessary costs.
   - o **Ensuring Security**: Observability helps detect unusual activity, such as unauthorized access attempts or suspicious traffic patterns.

Prometheus and Grafana: Setting up Basic Monitoring and Visualizing Data

Prometheus and **Grafana** are two popular open-source tools that work well together to provide detailed monitoring and visualization for Kubernetes.

1. **Prometheus**:
   - o **Role**: Prometheus is a powerful monitoring and alerting tool. It scrapes metrics from applications,

stores them in a time-series database, and can trigger alerts based on predefined thresholds.

- o **Architecture**:
  - Prometheus uses a pull-based model to scrape metrics from endpoints at regular intervals.
  - It supports querying with PromQL, Prometheus' custom query language, to filter and aggregate metrics.
- o **Kubernetes Metrics**:
  - In a Kubernetes environment, Prometheus scrapes metrics from the **Kube-State-Metrics**, **Node Exporter**, and application endpoints to monitor cluster and application health.

2. **Grafana**:
   - o **Role**: Grafana is a visualization tool that integrates with Prometheus to create dashboards for metrics visualization.
   - o **Dashboards and Alerts**:
     - Grafana allows you to create customizable dashboards, visualize complex data, and set up alert notifications based on metrics.
   - o **Integration with Prometheus**:

- Grafana connects to Prometheus as a data source, enabling users to query Prometheus metrics and visualize them in dashboards.

Practical Example: Configuring Prometheus and Grafana to Monitor a Sample Application

In this example, we'll set up Prometheus and Grafana in a Kubernetes cluster, configure them to monitor a sample web application, and create a dashboard to view the application's health metrics.

Step 1: Install Prometheus and Grafana in Kubernetes

1. **Install Prometheus and Grafana Using Helm**:
   - Helm is a package manager for Kubernetes that simplifies installing and managing applications like Prometheus and Grafana.
   - Add the Helm repository for Prometheus and Grafana:

   ```bash
   helm repo add prometheus-community https://prometheus-community.github.io/helm-charts
   helm repo add grafana https://grafana.github.io/helm-charts
   helm repo update
   ```

2. **Install Prometheus**:
   - Use Helm to install Prometheus with default configurations:

   bash
   helm install prometheus prometheus-community/kube-prometheus-stack

3. **Install Grafana**:
   - Use Helm to install Grafana:

   bash
   helm install grafana grafana/grafana

4. **Verify Installations**:
   - Check that Prometheus and Grafana pods are running:

   bash
   kubectl get pods -l app=prometheus
   kubectl get pods -l app.kubernetes.io/name=grafana

5. **Access Prometheus and Grafana Dashboards**:
   - By default, Grafana and Prometheus are accessible as services in the cluster. You can use kubectl port-forward to access them locally:

```bash
bash
kubectl port-forward svc/grafana 3000:80 &
kubectl port-forward svc/prometheus 9090:80 &
```

- o Access Grafana at http://localhost:3000 (default login: admin/prom-operator), and Prometheus at http://localhost:9090.

Step 2: Configure Prometheus to Monitor a Sample Application

1. **Deploy a Sample Application with Metrics**:
   - o We'll deploy a sample application (e.g., a simple Python or Node.js app) with metrics exposed at /metrics. Here's a sample deployment configuration:

```yaml
yaml
apiVersion: apps/v1
kind: Deployment
metadata:
  name: sample-app
  labels:
    app: sample-app
spec:
  replicas: 1
  selector:
    matchLabels:
```

```
       app: sample-app
    template:
     metadata:
      labels:
       app: sample-app
     spec:
      containers:
       - name: sample-app
         image: prom/prometheus-example-app:v0.1.0
         ports:
         - containerPort: 80
```

o   Save this as sample-app.yaml and deploy it:

bash
kubectl apply -f sample-app.yaml

2. **Expose the Application Metrics**:

o   Configure Prometheus to scrape metrics from the sample application by creating a **ServiceMonitor**. Here's an example configuration:

yaml
apiVersion: monitoring.coreos.com/v1
kind: ServiceMonitor
metadata:
 name: sample-app-monitor

```
labels:
  app: sample-app
spec:
 selector:
  matchLabels:
   app: sample-app
 endpoints:
 - port: metrics
  path: /metrics
```

- o Save this as sample-app-monitor.yaml and apply it:

bash

kubectl apply -f sample-app-monitor.yaml

3. **Verify Metrics in Prometheus**:
   - o Open Prometheus (http://localhost:9090), and use the **Status > Targets** page to check if Prometheus is successfully scraping metrics from the sample app.

Step 3: Set Up Grafana Dashboard to Visualize Metrics

1. **Add Prometheus as a Data Source in Grafana**:
   - o Go to http://localhost:3000 and log into Grafana.
   - o Navigate to **Configuration > Data Sources > Add data source**.
   - o Select **Prometheus** and enter the following URL:

vbnet

Copy code

http://prometheus-server.default.svc.cluster.local:9090

- o Save and test the data source to confirm connectivity.

2. **Create a Dashboard to Visualize Application Metrics**:
   - o In Grafana, navigate to **Create > Dashboard**.
   - o Add a new **Graph** panel and select **Prometheus** as the data source.
   - o Enter a sample query, such as http_requests_total (or similar metrics exposed by the sample app) to visualize incoming requests over time.

3. **Set Up Alerts in Grafana**:
   - o To receive notifications when metrics exceed specific thresholds, configure an alert on your dashboard panel.
   - o Example: Set an alert for high CPU usage by defining a threshold (e.g., rate(cpu_usage_seconds_total[5m]) > 0.8).

4. **Save the Dashboard**:
   - o Customize the dashboard by adding additional panels for metrics like memory usage, request latency, or error rates, then save the dashboard for ongoing monitoring.

In this chapter, we covered the basics of **Kubernetes observability** and highlighted the importance of monitoring key metrics such as resource utilization, application performance, and event logs. We introduced **Prometheus** for monitoring and **Grafana** for visualizing metrics and building dashboards. Through a practical example, we set up Prometheus and Grafana to monitor a sample application, configured Prometheus to scrape application metrics, and created a Grafana dashboard to visualize and set alerts on these metrics.

In the next chapter, we'll dive into **Debugging and Troubleshooting in Kubernetes**, where we'll look at tools and techniques for identifying and resolving issues within a Kubernetes environment

CHAPTER 13: DEBUGGING AND TROUBLESHOOTING IN KUBERNETES

Kubernetes environments are complex, and issues can arise at various levels—whether it's a pod that won't start, a deployment that isn't scaling correctly, or a configuration error that disrupts services. This chapter will cover common issues in Kubernetes, introduce useful **debugging tools and commands** like kubectl logs, kubectl describe, and kubectl exec, and walk through an example scenario of debugging a failing deployment.

Common Issues in Kubernetes: Pods, Deployments, and Configuration Problems

1. **Pod Issues**:
    - o **CrashLoopBackOff**: Indicates that a container within the pod is repeatedly crashing and restarting.
        - ▪ **Common Causes**: Application errors, incorrect image or tag, missing dependencies, or memory limits.
    - o **ImagePullBackOff**: The pod cannot pull the specified image from the registry.
        - ▪ **Common Causes**: Incorrect image name, tag, or registry credentials.
    - o **Pending**: The pod is created but cannot be scheduled to a node.

- **Common Causes**: Insufficient resources, such as CPU or memory, or missing volume configurations.
  - **OOMKilled**: The pod is terminated because it exceeded its memory limit.
    - **Common Causes**: Resource constraints, memory leaks, or insufficient memory allocation.

2. **Deployment Issues**:
   - **Unavailable Pods**: When desired replicas are not available.
     - **Common Causes**: Insufficient resources, failed readiness probes, or pod scheduling issues.
   - **Failed Rolling Update**: Rolling update stalls or fails to complete.
     - **Common Causes**: Misconfiguration in the deployment strategy, health checks failing, or incompatible configurations between versions.

3. **Configuration Problems**:
   - **Misconfigured Service**: Services may not route traffic correctly if selectors or ports are misconfigured.

- o **Incorrect Environment Variables**: Environment variables can affect application behavior; incorrect values can lead to failed deployments.
- o **Persistent Volume Claim (PVC) Issues**: PVCs may fail to bind if the requested storage is not available or incorrectly specified.

Debugging Tools and Commands: kubectl logs, kubectl describe, and kubectl exec

1. **kubectl logs**:
   - o The kubectl logs command retrieves logs from a container within a pod, which can provide insights into what went wrong.
   - o **Usage**:

     bash
     kubectl logs <pod-name>
     kubectl logs <pod-name> -c <container-name> # for multi-container pods

   - o **Common Use Cases**:
     - • Investigating application errors by checking the log output.
     - • Diagnosing issues like crash loops or initialization errors.

2. **kubectl describe**:

- o kubectl describe provides detailed information about a Kubernetes resource, including events, configurations, and error messages.
- o **Usage**:

bash
kubectl describe pod <pod-name>
kubectl describe deployment <deployment-name>

- o **Common Use Cases**:
  - ▪ Viewing events related to a pod, such as failed image pulls or health check failures.
  - ▪ Examining details about resource requests, limits, and configuration parameters for deployments, services, or pods.

3. **kubectl exec**:
  - o The kubectl exec command allows you to execute commands inside a running container, which is useful for inspecting files, running diagnostics, or troubleshooting connectivity.
  - o **Usage**:

bash
Copy code
kubectl exec -it <pod-name> -- /bin/sh   # Enter the shell of a container

kubectl exec <pod-name> -- <command>   # Run a specific command

- o **Common Use Cases**:
  - Inspecting configuration files within a container.
  - Testing network connectivity to other services within the cluster.
  - Running diagnostic commands, such as curl, ping, or top.

4. **kubectl get events**:
   - o Kubernetes events provide a chronological view of changes in resource states. kubectl get events lists recent events in the cluster, often showing issues like scheduling problems or image pull errors.
   - o **Usage**:

   bash
   kubectl   get   events   --sort-by='.metadata.creationTimestamp'

5. **kubectl port-forward**:
   - o kubectl port-forward creates a temporary connection to a Kubernetes service or pod for testing purposes. This is useful for debugging network access to an application.

o **Usage**:

bash
kubectl   port-forward   <pod-name>   <local-port>:<remote-port>

Example Scenario: Debugging a Failing Deployment and Common Fixes

In this example, we'll work through a scenario where a deployment fails, using kubectl commands to diagnose and address the issues.

Scenario Overview

Suppose you've deployed a web application, but the pods are stuck in CrashLoopBackOff and the deployment isn't scaling as expected. Let's troubleshoot and resolve these issues.

Step 1: Check the Status of the Deployment and Pods

1. **Get Deployment and Pod Status**:
   o Start by checking the status of the deployment and pods:

   bash
   kubectl get deployment web-app
   kubectl get pods -l app=web-app

2. **Inspect Pod Status**:

o If pods are in CrashLoopBackOff, note the pod names and move to the next steps.

1. **View Logs for the Failing Pod**:
    o Check logs to identify any error messages that might explain the crash:

    bash
    kubectl logs <pod-name>

    o **Example**:
       ▪ If the log shows a missing environment variable, you may see an error like:

       javascript
       Copy code
       Error: Missing environment variable DATABASE_URL

2. **Check Specific Containers** (for multi-container pods):
    o If the pod has multiple containers, specify the container name:

    bash
    kubectl logs <pod-name> -c <container-name>

Step 3: Use kubectl describe to Get Detailed Pod Information

1. **Describe the Failing Pod**:
   - Use kubectl describe to get detailed information about the pod, including events:

   bash
   kubectl describe pod <pod-name>

   - **Look for Event Messages**:
     - Common events include image pull errors, OOMKilled messages, or failed probes.
     - For example, if you see an ImagePullBackOff message, it could mean there's an issue with the image tag or repository permissions.

Step 4: Identify and Fix Configuration Issues

1. **Check Environment Variables**:
   - If the logs indicated a missing environment variable, review and update the deployment configuration.
   - Update the deployment YAML with the necessary environment variables:

   yaml
   apiVersion: apps/v1

```yaml
kind: Deployment
metadata:
  name: web-app
spec:
  replicas: 2
  selector:
    matchLabels:
      app: web-app
  template:
    metadata:
      labels:
        app: web-app
    spec:
      containers:
      - name: web-app-container
        image: my-web-app:latest
        env:
        - name: DATABASE_URL
          value:        "postgres://user:password@db-service:5432/db"
```

- o Apply the updated configuration:

bash

```bash
kubectl apply -f web-app-deployment.yaml
```

2. **Resolve Image Issues**:

   o If there's an image pull error, verify the image name and tag, or update the image registry credentials if needed.

3. **Adjust Resource Limits if Needed**:

   o If you noticed OOMKilled events, consider increasing memory limits:

   yaml

   ```
   resources:
     requests:
       memory: "128Mi"
     limits:
       memory: "256Mi"
   ```

Step 5: Test Network Connectivity with kubectl exec

1. **Enter the Pod's Shell**:

   o Use kubectl exec to enter the pod and test network connectivity:

   bash
   ```
   kubectl exec -it <pod-name> -- /bin/sh
   ```

2. **Test Connectivity to Other Services**:

- o For example, if the application depends on a database service, use ping or curl to test connectivity:

```bash
curl http://db-service:5432
```

Step 6: Verify Fixes and Monitor Events

1. **Check Pod and Deployment Status**:
   - o After making changes, confirm that the deployment and pods are running successfully:

```bash
kubectl get deployment web-app
kubectl get pods -l app=web-app
```

2. **Monitor Events**:
   - o Use kubectl get events to check for any new issues:

```bash
kubectl get events --sort-by='.metadata.creationTimestamp'
```

In this chapter, we explored common issues in Kubernetes, including pod and deployment problems, as well as configuration errors. We covered essential **debugging commands** like kubectl logs, kubectl describe, and kubectl exec, which help diagnose and troubleshoot issues in Kubernetes environments. Finally, we walked through an example scenario of debugging a failing deployment and using kubectl commands to investigate, correct, and verify fixes.

In the next chapter, we'll cover **Security Best Practices in Kubernetes**, where we'll look at strategies for securing applications, managing access, and protecting sensitive data within Kubernetes clusters.

CHAPTER 14: KUBERNETES SECURITY ESSENTIALS

Securing a Kubernetes cluster requires a layered approach that protects resources, controls access, and manages sensitive information effectively. In this chapter, we'll explore **Kubernetes security fundamentals**, covering topics like **Role-Based Access Control (RBAC)**, **network policies**, and best practices for securing clusters. We'll also provide a real-world example of implementing basic RBAC policies for different users.

Understanding Kubernetes Security: Role-Based Access Control (RBAC) and Network Policies

1. **Role-Based Access Control (RBAC):**
   o **What is RBAC?**
      ▪ **RBAC** is a Kubernetes feature that restricts access to resources based on roles and permissions. It allows administrators to define who can access specific resources and what actions they can perform.
      ▪ By defining **roles** (permissions associated with actions) and **role bindings** (assigning roles to users or groups), you can control access to cluster resources at a granular level.
   o **Key Components of RBAC:**

- **Role**: Defines a set of permissions for a namespace (e.g., allowing read access to all pods).
- **ClusterRole**: Defines permissions at the cluster level (e.g., granting permissions to manage nodes or create namespaces).
- **RoleBinding**: Associates a role with users or groups within a namespace.
- **ClusterRoleBinding**: Associates a ClusterRole with users or groups at the cluster level.

o **Example RBAC Configuration**:
  - This example allows a specific user to view resources within a namespace:

```yaml
apiVersion: rbac.authorization.k8s.io/v1
kind: Role
metadata:
  namespace: development
  name: view-only
rules:
- apiGroups: [""]
  resources: ["pods", "services"]
  verbs: ["get", "list"]
```
yaml

```
Copy code
apiVersion: rbac.authorization.k8s.io/v1
kind: RoleBinding
metadata:
  name: view-only-binding
  namespace: development
subjects:
- kind: User
  name: alice
  apiGroup: rbac.authorization.k8s.io
roleRef:
  kind: Role
  name: view-only
  apiGroup: rbac.authorization.k8s.io
```

- **Benefits of RBAC**:
  - **Improves Security**: Minimizes access by following the principle of least privilege.
  - **Enhances Compliance**: Helps enforce access policies and comply with security standards.
  - **Reduces Human Error**: Restricts users to specific actions, reducing the risk of unintended changes.

2. **Network Policies**:
   - **What are Network Policies?**

- **Network policies** control communication between pods and network endpoints. They define rules to allow or deny traffic between pods based on labels and namespaces.

o **Components of a Network Policy**:
  - **Pod Selector**: Specifies which pods the policy applies to.
  - **Ingress and Egress Rules**: Define allowed inbound and outbound traffic, respectively.
  - **Namespace Selector**: Specifies namespaces affected by the policy.

o **Example Network Policy**:
  - The following network policy allows inbound traffic to pods labeled app: web only from pods labeled app: frontend:

```yaml
apiVersion: networking.k8s.io/v1
kind: NetworkPolicy
metadata:
  name: web-allow-frontend
  namespace: production
spec:
  podSelector:
    matchLabels:
      app: web
```

```
ingress:
- from:
  - podSelector:
    matchLabels:
      app: frontend
```

- o **Benefits of Network Policies**:
  - **Limits Unwanted Communication**: Prevents unauthorized access to services by isolating pods.
  - **Enhances Security**: Enforces communication boundaries, making it harder for malicious users or compromised services to access other pods.

Best Practices for Securing Clusters: Pod Security, API Server Access, and Secrets Management

1. **Pod Security**:
   - o **Pod Security Policies (PSP)**: Deprecated in recent Kubernetes versions, but some clusters still use PSPs to enforce security standards for pods.
   - o **Pod Security Admission (PSA)**: Replaces PSP with three levels—**privileged**, **baseline**, and **restricted**—to define allowed behaviors within a cluster.

- o **Best Practices for Pod Security**:
  - ▪ **Run Containers as Non-Root**: Prevents containers from having root access, reducing the risk of privilege escalation.
  - ▪ **Use Read-Only Root Filesystems**: Limits the ability to modify the filesystem within the container, enhancing security.
  - ▪ **Set Resource Limits**: Define CPU and memory limits to prevent resource exhaustion.

2. **API Server Access**:
   - o **Restrict API Server Access**:
     - ▪ Limit access to the Kubernetes API server by using secure authentication methods (e.g., certificates or tokens) and restricting external access via firewall rules.
   - o **Enable Auditing**:
     - ▪ Enable API auditing to log access attempts and actions performed via the API server. This provides a record of all interactions, which can be useful for compliance and security investigations.

3. **Secrets Management**:
   - o **What are Secrets?**

- Kubernetes Secrets are objects used to store sensitive information, like passwords, API keys, and certificates, that pods can access securely.
  - **Best Practices for Managing Secrets**:
    - **Limit Access to Secrets**: Use RBAC to restrict access to secrets, ensuring only authorized services can access them.
    - **Use Encryption**: Enable encryption at rest for secrets to prevent unauthorized access to sensitive information.
    - **Use External Secret Managers**: Consider using external tools like HashiCorp Vault, AWS Secrets Manager, or Azure Key Vault for added security.

Real-World Application: Implementing Basic RBAC Policies for Different Users

In this example, we'll set up basic RBAC policies to manage access for three different users: alice, bob, and charlie. Each user will have different levels of access within a development namespace.

Scenario Overview

- **alice**: A developer who needs to view all resources in the development namespace.
- **bob**: A DevOps engineer with permission to view, create, and update resources.
- **charlie**: A project manager who only needs read-only access to view deployments and services.

1. **Define the Development Namespace**:
   - First, create a namespace called development to organize resources for this example:

   yaml
   apiVersion: v1
   kind: Namespace
   metadata:
     name: development

   - Apply the configuration:

   bash
   kubectl apply -f development-namespace.yaml

1. **RBAC Policy for alice (View-Only Access)**:

o   Define a role with view-only access to all resources in the development namespace:

yaml
Copy code

```
apiVersion: rbac.authorization.k8s.io/v1
kind: Role
metadata:
  namespace: development
  name: view-only
rules:
- apiGroups: [""]
  resources: ["pods", "services", "configmaps"]
  verbs: ["get", "list"]
```

o   Bind the role to alice:

yaml

```
apiVersion: rbac.authorization.k8s.io/v1
kind: RoleBinding
metadata:
  name: view-only-binding
  namespace: development
subjects:
- kind: User
  name: alice
```

apiGroup: rbac.authorization.k8s.io

roleRef:

  kind: Role

  name: view-only

  apiGroup: rbac.authorization.k8s.io

2. **RBAC Policy for bob (Read and Write Access)**:

  o Define a role allowing bob to view, create, and update resources:

```yaml
apiVersion: rbac.authorization.k8s.io/v1
kind: Role
metadata:
  namespace: development
  name: read-write
rules:
- apiGroups: [""]
  resources: ["pods", "services", "configmaps", "deployments"]
  verbs: ["get", "list", "create", "update", "patch"]
```

  o Bind the role to bob:

```yaml
apiVersion: rbac.authorization.k8s.io/v1
kind: RoleBinding
```

```yaml
metadata:
  name: read-write-binding
  namespace: development
subjects:
- kind: User
  name: bob
  apiGroup: rbac.authorization.k8s.io
roleRef:
  kind: Role
  name: read-write
  apiGroup: rbac.authorization.k8s.io
```

3. **RBAC Policy for charlie (Limited View Access)**:
   - Define a role that only grants charlie permission to view deployments and services:

```yaml
yaml
apiVersion: rbac.authorization.k8s.io/v1
kind: Role
metadata:
  namespace: development
  name: limited-view
rules:
- apiGroups: [""]
  resources: ["deployments", "services"]
  verbs: ["get", "list"]
```

o Bind the role to charlie:

```yaml
apiVersion: rbac.authorization.k8s.io/v1
kind: RoleBinding
metadata:
  name: limited-view-binding
  namespace: development
subjects:
- kind: User
  name: charlie
  apiGroup: rbac.authorization.k8s.io
roleRef:
  kind: Role
  name: limited-view
  apiGroup: rbac.authorization.k8s.io
```

Step 3: Apply the RBAC Policies

1. **Apply All Configurations**:
   o Save each configuration as YAML files and apply them to the cluster:

```bash
kubectl apply -f alice-view-only.yaml
kubectl apply -f bob-read-write.yaml
kubectl apply -f charlie-limited-view.yaml
```

2. **Verify Access**:

    o   Test each user's permissions to confirm they can only access resources as specified by the RBAC policies.

In this chapter, we explored essential Kubernetes security concepts, focusing on **Role-Based Access Control (RBAC)** and **network policies**. We discussed best practices for securing clusters, including pod security, API server access, and secrets management. Through a real-world example, we implemented RBAC policies for different users, demonstrating how to control access based on roles.

In the next chapter, we'll cover **CI/CD Pipelines in Kubernetes**, where we'll look at setting up continuous integration and deployment for Kubernetes applications.

CHAPTER 15: CI/CD WITH KUBERNETES

Implementing **Continuous Integration and Continuous Deployment (CI/CD)** pipelines in Kubernetes enhances the efficiency, reliability, and speed of application delivery. This chapter covers how to set up CI/CD pipelines in Kubernetes using tools like **Jenkins**, **GitLab CI**, or **GitHub Actions** and demonstrates how to automate deployments using techniques such as rolling updates and canary deployments. Finally, we'll walk through an example of configuring a CI/CD pipeline to deploy a simple application to Kubernetes.

Setting Up CI/CD Pipelines: Integrating Kubernetes with Jenkins, GitLab, or GitHub Actions

1. **Continuous Integration (CI)**:
    o CI focuses on automatically building and testing code each time a developer pushes changes to a repository. Automated testing helps identify and fix issues early, ensuring high code quality before deployment.
    o Popular CI tools for Kubernetes:
        ▪ **Jenkins**: A widely used open-source CI tool that can be integrated with Kubernetes for building, testing, and deploying applications.
        ▪ **GitLab CI**: An integrated CI/CD solution available with GitLab that simplifies setting up pipelines with Kubernetes integrations.
        ▪ **GitHub Actions**: A GitHub-integrated CI/CD tool that can deploy to Kubernetes

clusters and automate testing, building, and deployment workflows.

2. **Continuous Deployment (CD)**:

   o CD automates the process of deploying code changes to production or staging environments after passing CI checks. This allows teams to deploy updates frequently and reliably.

   o **Benefits of CI/CD in Kubernetes**:

      ▪ **Accelerates Release Cycles**: With automated testing and deployment, teams can release updates quickly.

      ▪ **Reduces Human Error**: Automation minimizes manual intervention, reducing the risk of errors.

      ▪ **Improves Collaboration**: CI/CD standardizes the process for releasing software, making it easier for teams to collaborate.

3. **Example CI/CD Tool Integrations**:

   o **Jenkins**:

      ▪ Jenkins can run in a Kubernetes cluster and use Kubernetes plugins to dynamically provision build agents as pods.

      ▪ Configure pipelines using **Jenkinsfiles** to define the build, test, and deployment stages.

- o **GitLab CI**:
  - GitLab CI can be configured with a .gitlab-ci.yml file, which defines the pipeline stages and jobs.
  - Built-in integrations with Kubernetes allow seamless deployment to clusters.
- o **GitHub Actions**:
  - With GitHub Actions, workflows are defined in .yml files in the .github/workflows directory.
  - Kubernetes deployment actions enable GitHub Actions to interact with clusters and deploy applications.

utomating Deployments: Rolling Updates and Canary Deployments

1. **Rolling Updates**:
   - o **Definition**: Rolling updates gradually replace old pods with new ones, ensuring zero downtime and allowing the application to serve traffic without interruption.
   - o **How it Works**:
     - Kubernetes deployments use rolling updates by default, creating new pods while gradually terminating the old ones.

- You can specify **maxUnavailable** and **maxSurge** options to control the update speed.
  - **Example Rolling Update Configuration**:
    - In the deployment YAML file, specify the update strategy:

```yaml
Copy code
strategy:
  type: RollingUpdate
  rollingUpdate:
    maxUnavailable: 1
    maxSurge: 1
```

2. **Canary Deployments**:
   - **Definition**: Canary deployments release new application versions to a small subset of users before full rollout, reducing risk by testing changes with a limited audience.
   - **How it Works**:
     - Create two deployments for the application: one with the current stable version and another with the canary version.

- Use services or ingress rules to route a small percentage of traffic to the canary deployment.
  o **Example Canary Deployment Setup**:
    - Deploy the canary version with fewer replicas:

```yaml
Copy code
apiVersion: apps/v1
kind: Deployment
metadata:
  name: app-canary
spec:
  replicas: 1
  selector:
    matchLabels:
      app: myapp
      version: canary
  template:
    metadata:
      labels:
        app: myapp
        version: canary
    spec:
      containers:
```

```
- name: myapp
  image: myapp:v2.0
```

- o **Managing Traffic to the Canary**:
  - Use a weighted load balancer, service mesh (e.g., Istio), or ingress configuration to route a small percentage of traffic to the canary deployment.

Example: Configuring a CI/CD Pipeline to Deploy a Simple Application to Kubernetes

In this example, we'll configure a CI/CD pipeline using **GitHub Actions** to automate the deployment of a sample application to a Kubernetes cluster.

Step 1: Set Up Kubernetes Access in GitHub Actions

1. **Create a Service Account and Role Binding in Kubernetes**:
   - o Define a service account in Kubernetes with access to deploy to the cluster:

   ```yaml
   Copy code
   apiVersion: v1
   kind: ServiceAccount
   metadata:
   ```

```
    name: github-actions
    namespace: default
```

o   Bind this service account to a role with necessary permissions:

```yaml
Copy code
apiVersion: rbac.authorization.k8s.io/v1
kind: RoleBinding
metadata:
  name: github-actions-binding
  namespace: default
subjects:
- kind: ServiceAccount
  name: github-actions
  namespace: default
roleRef:
  kind: ClusterRole
  name: cluster-admin  # Replace with specific roles for tighter security
  apiGroup: rbac.authorization.k8s.io
```

o   Apply these configurations:

```bash
Copy code
```

```
kubectl apply -f service-account.yaml
kubectl apply -f role-binding.yaml
```

2. **Configure GitHub Secrets**:

   o Retrieve the Kubernetes configuration file (kubeconfig) for the service account and store it as a secret in your GitHub repository:

   bash
   Copy code
   ```
   kubectl config view --flatten --minify > kubeconfig.yaml
   ```

   o Go to **Settings > Secrets** in your GitHub repository and add the kubeconfig as a secret named KUBE_CONFIG.

Step 2: Define the CI/CD Pipeline in GitHub Actions

1. **Create a Workflow File**:

   o In your repository, create a .github/workflows/deploy.yml file to define the deployment pipeline.

2. **Define the Workflow Steps**:

   o Here's an example GitHub Actions workflow that builds a Docker image, pushes it to Docker Hub, and deploys it to Kubernetes:

```yaml
Copy code
name: CI/CD Pipeline

on:
  push:
    branches:
      - main

jobs:
  build-and-deploy:
    runs-on: ubuntu-latest
    env:
      DOCKER_USERNAME: ${{ secrets.DOCKER_USERNAME }}
      DOCKER_PASSWORD: ${{ secrets.DOCKER_PASSWORD }}
      KUBE_CONFIG: ${{ secrets.KUBE_CONFIG }}
      IMAGE_NAME: myapp
      IMAGE_TAG: latest

    steps:
      - name: Checkout code
        uses: actions/checkout@v2
```

```yaml
- name: Log in to Docker Hub
  run: echo $DOCKER_PASSWORD | docker login -u $DOCKER_USERNAME --password-stdin

- name: Build Docker image
  run: docker build -t $DOCKER_USERNAME/$IMAGE_NAME:$IMAGE_TAG .

- name: Push Docker image
  run: docker push $DOCKER_USERNAME/$IMAGE_NAME:$IMAGE_TAG

- name: Set up Kubernetes
  uses: azure/setup-kubectl@v1
  with:
    kubeconfig: ${{ secrets.KUBE_CONFIG }}

- name: Deploy to Kubernetes
  run: |
    kubectl set image deployment/myapp myapp=$DOCKER_USERNAME/$IMAGE_NAME:$IMAGE_TAG
```

- o **Explanation**:
  - • **Checkout code**: Pulls the latest code from the repository.
  - • **Log in to Docker Hub**: Authenticates to Docker Hub using secrets.
  - • **Build Docker image**: Builds a Docker image from the code.
  - • **Push Docker image**: Pushes the image to Docker Hub.
  - • **Set up Kubernetes**: Configures kubectl with the kubeconfig secret.
  - • **Deploy to Kubernetes**: Updates the deployment image with the new version.

3. **Apply the Deployment in Kubernetes**:
   - o Define the deployment YAML in Kubernetes for myapp, which GitHub Actions will update:

```yaml
Copy code
apiVersion: apps/v1
kind: Deployment
metadata:
  name: myapp
  namespace: default
spec:
  replicas: 2
```

```
selector:
  matchLabels:
    app: myapp
template:
  metadata:
    labels:
      app: myapp
  spec:
    containers:
    - name: myapp
      image: myapp:latest
```

o   Apply the deployment file to the cluster:

bash

Copy code

kubectl apply -f myapp-deployment.yaml

Step 3: Test the CI/CD Pipeline

1. **Push Changes to GitHub**:
   - o   Push changes to the main branch, and the GitHub Actions pipeline will automatically start, building, pushing, and deploying the updated application.

2. **Monitor the Deployment**:
   - o   Use kubectl commands to verify the deployment in Kubernetes:

bash

Copy code

kubectl get pods

kubectl get deployments

3. **Verify Application Update**:
   o Ensure the updated version is deployed by checking the application's status or logs.

In this chapter, we explored how to set up **CI/CD pipelines** for Kubernetes using popular tools like **Jenkins**, **GitLab CI**, and **GitHub Actions**. We discussed **rolling updates** and **canary deployments** as strategies for automating application updates with minimal disruption. The example demonstrated a complete GitHub Actions CI/CD pipeline that builds, pushes, and deploys a sample application to Kubernetes, providing a streamlined workflow for continuous delivery.

In the next chapter, we'll discuss **Managing Stateful Applications and Databases in Kubernetes**, covering best practices and tools for handling persistent data and stateful workloads.

CHAPTER 16: HELM AND KUBERNETES PACKAGE MANAGEMENT

Helm is the leading package manager for Kubernetes, making it easier to deploy, manage, and version applications. In this chapter, we'll cover why Helm has become essential for Kubernetes package management, how to create and deploy Helm charts to manage application versions and configurations, and walk through a practical example of building a Helm chart for a web application.

Introduction to Helm: Why Helm is the Package Manager for Kubernetes

1. **What is Helm?**

   o **Helm** is a package manager for Kubernetes that allows you to define, install, and upgrade complex Kubernetes applications. Helm packages applications into **charts**—collections of YAML files that define a set of Kubernetes resources.

   o Helm charts act like application templates, making it easy to deploy applications with a standard configuration across multiple environments (e.g., development, staging, production).

2. **Why Use Helm?**

   o **Simplifies Deployment**: Helm automates the process of deploying, upgrading, and managing applications in Kubernetes, reducing the need for manual configuration and repetitive YAML files.

   o **Centralized Configuration Management**: Helm charts enable you to store configuration parameters in a single file, which makes it easy to manage application versions and configurations consistently.

   o **Version Control and Rollbacks**: Helm maintains a history of application deployments, enabling you to easily roll back to a previous version if needed.

   o **Reusable and Shareable Charts**: Helm charts can be shared publicly or privately, making it easy to deploy common applications and configurations across multiple projects or teams.

3. **Key Components of Helm**:

   o **Helm CLI**: The command-line tool that manages Helm charts, releases, and repositories.

   o **Chart**: A Helm package that contains templates, values, and metadata for deploying applications.

   o **Release**: An instance of a Helm chart deployed to a Kubernetes cluster. Each release has a unique name, enabling you to deploy multiple instances of the same chart.

   o **Values File**: A YAML file that holds configuration values used to customize the Helm chart during deployment.

Creating and Deploying Helm Charts: How to Manage Application Versions and Configurations

1. **Creating a Helm Chart**:

   o Helm provides a simple way to create a new chart using the helm create command, which scaffolds the necessary directory structure and files for a basic chart.

   bash
   helm create myapp

- o This command generates a chart directory (myapp) with the following structure:

bash

myapp/

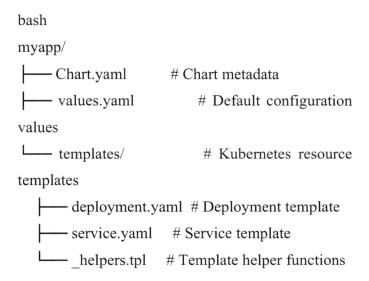

├── Chart.yaml   # Chart metadata

├── values.yaml   # Default configuration values

└── templates/   # Kubernetes resource templates

├── deployment.yaml # Deployment template

├── service.yaml   # Service template

└── _helpers.tpl   # Template helper functions

2. **Configuring the Chart**:
    - o **Chart.yaml**: Contains metadata for the chart, such as its name, version, and description.

yaml

apiVersion: v2

name: myapp

version: 0.1.0

description: A Helm chart for my web application

- o **values.yaml**: Stores default values for variables used in templates. These values can be overridden during deployment.

```yaml
yaml
replicaCount: 2
image:
  repository: nginx
  tag: "1.19.6"
service:
  type: ClusterIP
  port: 80
```

o **Templates**: YAML files in the templates directory define the Kubernetes resources (e.g., Deployment, Service) for the application. Helm replaces placeholders with values from values.yaml.

Example deployment.yaml template:

```yaml
yaml
apiVersion: apps/v1
kind: Deployment
metadata:
  name: {{ .Release.Name }}-{{ .Chart.Name }}
spec:
  replicas: {{ .Values.replicaCount }}
  selector:
    matchLabels:
      app: {{ .Release.Name }}-{{ .Chart.Name }}
```

```
template:
 metadata:
  labels:
   app: {{ .Release.Name }}-{{ .Chart.Name }}
  spec:
  containers:
  - name: {{ .Chart.Name }}
   image: "{{ .Values.image.repository }}:{{
.Values.image.tag }}"
   ports:
   - containerPort: {{ .Values.service.port }}
```

- o **Template Variables**:
    - **{{ .Release.Name }}**: Automatically inserts the release name.
    - **{{ .Values.<parameter> }}**: Inserts values from values.yaml.

3. **Installing a Helm Chart**:
   - o Once the chart is configured, use the helm install command to deploy it to Kubernetes.

   bash
   helm install myapp ./myapp

   - o **Explanation**:

- myapp is the release name, and ./myapp is the chart directory.
  - **Customizing Installation**:
    - Override default values by passing a custom values file:

      bash

      helm install myapp ./myapp -f custom-values.yaml

4. **Upgrading and Rolling Back Releases**:
   - **Upgrade**: Update a release with new chart values or configurations:

     bash

     helm upgrade myapp ./myapp -f updated-values.yaml

   - **Rollback**: Revert a release to a previous version:

     bash

     helm rollback myapp <revision>

   - **List Previous Versions**:

     bash

     helm history myapp

Example Project: Building a Helm Chart for a Web Application

Let's create a Helm chart to deploy a simple web application (e.g., an NGINX server) and customize the deployment by setting values for replicas, image version, and service type.

Step 1: Create the Helm Chart

1. **Generate the Chart**:
   - o Run the helm create command to scaffold a new chart:

   bash
   helm create webapp

2. **Edit the Chart Metadata**:
   - o Open webapp/Chart.yaml and modify the chart details:

   yaml
   Copy code
   apiVersion: v2
   name: webapp
   version: 0.1.0
   description: A Helm chart for a simple NGINX web application

Step 2: Configure Default Values in values.yaml

1. **Set Default Values**:
    - Open webapp/values.yaml and configure the application parameters:

    ```yaml
    yaml
    replicaCount: 2
    image:
      repository: nginx
      tag: "1.19.6"
      pullPolicy: IfNotPresent
    service:
      type: LoadBalancer
      port: 80
    ```

2. **Explanation of Parameters**:
    - replicaCount: Sets the number of pod replicas.
    - image: Defines the container image and version.
    - service: Configures the service type (LoadBalancer in this case) and port.

Step 3: Customize the Deployment Template

1. **Edit deployment.yaml**:
    - Modify webapp/templates/deployment.yaml to use the values from values.yaml:

    ```yaml
    yaml
    ```

```
apiVersion: apps/v1
kind: Deployment
metadata:
  name: {{ .Release.Name }}-{{ .Chart.Name }}
  labels:
    app: {{ .Release.Name }}-{{ .Chart.Name }}
spec:
  replicas: {{ .Values.replicaCount }}
  selector:
    matchLabels:
      app: {{ .Release.Name }}-{{ .Chart.Name }}
  template:
    metadata:
      labels:
        app: {{ .Release.Name }}-{{ .Chart.Name }}
    spec:
      containers:
      - name: {{ .Chart.Name }}
        image: "{{ .Values.image.repository }}:{{ .Values.image.tag }}"
        ports:
        - containerPort: {{ .Values.service.port }}
```

2. **Explanation of Template Variables**:

   o **{{ .Values.<parameter> }}**: Replaces placeholders with values from values.yaml.

- o **{{ .Release.Name }}**: Inserts the release name, making the deployment unique for each release.

Step 4: Deploy the Helm Chart to Kubernetes

1. **Install the Chart**:
   - o Deploy the chart with a custom release name:

   bash
   helm install webapp-release ./webapp

2. **Verify the Deployment**:
   - o Check the status of the Helm release:

   bash
   helm status webapp-release

   - o Use kubectl commands to verify that the pods and services are running:

   bash
   kubectl get pods
   kubectl get svc

Step 5: Upgrade the Helm Chart

1. **Update values.yaml for a New Version**:

o Change the image tag in values.yaml to upgrade the application version:

yaml

Copy code

```
image:
  repository: nginx
  tag: "1.20.1"
```

2. **Apply the Upgrade**:

o Use helm upgrade to apply the new configuration:

bash

Copy code

```
helm upgrade webapp-release ./webapp
```

3. **Verify the Upgrade**:

o Check the release status and confirm the new version is deployed:

bash

```
helm status webapp-release
```

4. **Rollback if Needed**:

o If the upgrade causes issues, roll back to the previous version:

bash

helm rollback webapp-release <revision>

In this chapter, we explored **Helm** as the package manager for Kubernetes, learning how it simplifies application deployment, configuration management, and version control. We covered the components of a Helm chart, how to customize deployments with values files, and how to manage application versions and rollbacks. Through a practical example, we created a Helm chart for a web application, deployed it to Kubernetes, upgraded it, and performed a rollback.

In the next chapter, we'll dive into **Managing Stateful Applications and Databases in Kubernetes**, where we'll explore best practices for handling persistent data and managing stateful workloads.

CHAPTER 17: ADVANCED SCHEDULING IN KUBERNETES

Kubernetes uses a scheduler to determine the optimal placement of pods across nodes, but you can control this placement to suit specific workload requirements. Advanced scheduling techniques like **Node Affinity and Anti-Affinity** and **Taints and Tolerations** allow you to fine-tune where workloads run within the cluster, enhancing performance, availability, and isolation. In this chapter, we'll explore these scheduling mechanisms and walk through a real-world example of using affinity and tolerations to optimize workloads in a multi-zone cluster.

Node Affinity and Anti-Affinity: Controlling Where Pods are Placed

1. **What is Node Affinity?**
   - o **Node Affinity** allows you to specify rules that determine which nodes a pod should or should not be scheduled on. These rules are based on node labels and can either **require** or **prefer** a pod to be placed on certain nodes.
   - o **Types of Node Affinity**:
     - ▪ **requiredDuringSchedulingIgnoredDuring Execution**: The pod **must** be placed on a node that matches the rule.
     - ▪ **preferredDuringSchedulingIgnoredDurin gExecution**: The pod **prefers** nodes that match the rule, but it can be scheduled elsewhere if needed.

2. **Example of Node Affinity**:
   - o Suppose you have nodes labeled by availability zone, and you want a pod to run only in the us-west zone:

```yaml
affinity:
  nodeAffinity:

    requiredDuringSchedulingIgnoredDuringExecution:
      nodeSelectorTerms:
      - matchExpressions:
        - key: topology.kubernetes.io/zone
          operator: In
          values:
          - us-west
```

3. **Node Anti-Affinity**:
   o **Node Anti-Affinity** allows you to specify that certain pods should **not** be scheduled on the same node or in proximity to other pods with matching labels. This is often used to spread out replicas for high availability.
   o **Example of Node Anti-Affinity**:
      ▪ For example, if you have multiple replicas of a critical service and want to ensure they aren't placed on the same node:

```yaml
affinity:
  podAntiAffinity:
```

```
requiredDuringSchedulingIgnoredDuringEx
ecution:
  - labelSelector:
    matchExpressions:
    - key: app
      operator: In
      values:
      - critical-service
    topologyKey: "kubernetes.io/hostname"
```

- o **Explanation**:
  - ▪ The podAntiAffinity rule ensures that no two pods labeled with app: critical-service are placed on the same node, improving redundancy.

4. **Use Cases for Affinity and Anti-Affinity**:
   - o **High Availability**: Distribute replicas across nodes to avoid a single point of failure.
   - o **Resource Optimization**: Schedule high-performance workloads on nodes with more resources.
   - o **Data Locality**: Ensure data-processing workloads are scheduled closer to storage nodes or zones.

Taints and Tolerations: Keeping Certain Workloads Isolated

1. **What are Taints?**
   o **Taints** are applied to nodes to repel certain pods, ensuring that only pods with matching tolerations can be scheduled on those nodes. Taints can prevent regular workloads from being scheduled on specific nodes, like those reserved for specialized tasks.

2. **Applying Taints to Nodes**:
   o You can add a taint to a node using the kubectl taint command:

   bash
   kubectl taint nodes <node-name> key=value:effect

   o **Effects**:
      ▪ **NoSchedule**: Prevents pods without a matching toleration from being scheduled on the node.
      ▪ **PreferNoSchedule**: Prefers not to schedule pods without a matching toleration on the node but won't enforce it strictly.
      ▪ **NoExecute**: Evicts pods from the node unless they have a matching toleration.

3. **What are Tolerations?**
   o **Tolerations** allow pods to be scheduled on nodes with matching taints. A pod with a toleration will

"tolerate" the taint on a node, allowing it to be scheduled there.

4. **Example of Taints and Tolerations**:
   - ○ Let's say you have GPU nodes in your cluster, and you want only GPU workloads to run on those nodes:
   - ○ **Apply a Taint to the GPU Node**:

   bash

   kubectl taint nodes gpu-node gpu=true:NoSchedule

   - ○ **Add a Toleration to GPU Workloads**:
     - ▪ In the pod spec, add a toleration so that only pods with this toleration can run on the GPU node:

     yaml

     tolerations:

     - key: "gpu"

       operator: "Equal"

       value: "true"

       effect: "NoSchedule"

5. **Use Cases for Taints and Tolerations**:
   - ○ **Workload Isolation**: Restrict certain workloads to dedicated nodes (e.g., GPU or high-memory nodes).

- o **Failure Isolation**: Keep critical workloads away from unstable or heavily loaded nodes.
- o **Multi-Tenant Clusters**: Use taints to keep workloads from different teams isolated within shared clusters.

Real-world Example: Using Affinity and Tolerations to Optimize Workloads in a Multi-Zone Cluster

In this example, we'll optimize workload scheduling in a Kubernetes cluster that spans multiple availability zones (e.g., us-west and us-east). The goal is to use node affinity to ensure that latency-sensitive applications are located in the same zone and use taints to reserve specific nodes for critical workloads.

Scenario Overview

- The cluster is deployed in two zones: us-west and us-east.
- **Web App Pods**: Low-latency applications that need to be placed in the us-west zone for proximity to user data.
- **Database Pods**: Critical workloads that should be isolated on high-memory nodes reserved specifically for database operations.

Step 1: Apply Node Labels for Zones and Database Nodes

1. **Label Nodes by Zone**:

o Label nodes in the us-west and us-east zones for affinity-based scheduling:

bash
kubectl label nodes <us-west-node-1> topology.kubernetes.io/zone=us-west
kubectl label nodes <us-east-node-1> topology.kubernetes.io/zone=us-east

2. **Label High-Memory Nodes for Database Use**:
   o Label nodes with high memory for database workloads:

bash
Copy code
kubectl label nodes <db-node-1> high-memory=true

Step 2: Use Node Affinity for Web App Pods

1. **Define Node Affinity in the Web App Deployment**:
   o Configure node affinity to ensure the Web App pods are scheduled in the us-west zone:

yaml
apiVersion: apps/v1
kind: Deployment

```yaml
metadata:
  name: web-app
spec:
  replicas: 3
  selector:
    matchLabels:
      app: web-app
  template:
    metadata:
      labels:
        app: web-app
    spec:
      affinity:
        nodeAffinity:

          requiredDuringSchedulingIgnoredDuringExecution:
            nodeSelectorTerms:
            - matchExpressions:
              - key: topology.kubernetes.io/zone
                operator: In
                values:
                - us-west
      containers:
      - name: web-app
        image: nginx
```

ports:

- containerPort: 80

2. **Deploy the Web App**:

   o   Apply the deployment configuration:

   bash

   kubectl apply -f web-app-deployment.yaml

Step 3: Apply Taints and Tolerations for Database Pods

1. **Taint the High-Memory Database Node**:

   o   Add a taint to the high-memory node to reserve it for database pods:

   bash

   kubectl   taint   nodes   <db-node-1>   high-memory=true:NoSchedule

2. **Add Tolerations for Database Pods**:

   o   In the database deployment configuration, add a toleration to allow these pods to be scheduled on the tainted high-memory node:

   yaml

   Copy code

   apiVersion: apps/v1

   kind: Deployment

```
    metadata:
     name: db-app
    spec:
     replicas: 1
     selector:
      matchLabels:
       app: db-app
     template:
      metadata:
       labels:
        app: db-app
     spec:
      tolerations:
      - key: "high-memory"
       operator: "Equal"
       value: "true"
       effect: "NoSchedule"
      containers:
      - name: db-app
       image: postgres
       ports:
       - containerPort: 5432
```

3. **Deploy the Database Pods**:
   o   Apply the database deployment:

bash

Copy code

kubectl apply -f db-app-deployment.yaml

Step 4: Verify Pod Placement

1. **Check Web App Pod Placement**:
   - Ensure that all web-app pods are placed in nodes labeled with us-west:

   bash

   Copy code

   kubectl get pods -o wide -l app=web-app

2. **Check Database Pod Placement**:
   - Verify that db-app pods are placed only on nodes with the high-memory=true taint:

   bash

   Copy code

   kubectl get pods -o wide -l app=db-app

In this chapter, we explored advanced scheduling in Kubernetes, focusing on **Node Affinity and Anti-Affinity** and **Taints and Tolerations**. We discussed how to use node affinity to control where pods are scheduled based on node labels and node anti-affinity to spread out replicas for high availability. Taints and tolerations allow you to isolate specific workloads to dedicated nodes, helping improve performance and resource utilization. Through a real-world example, we used affinity and tolerations to optimize workload placement in a multi-zone cluster.

In the next chapter, we'll discuss **Stateful Applications and Databases in Kubernetes**, where we'll cover best practices for managing persistent data and deploying stateful workloads

CHAPTER 18: KUBERNETES IN PRODUCTION

Running Kubernetes in a production environment requires advanced strategies for **cluster management and scaling, handling node failures**, and **ensuring high availability**. In this chapter, we'll explore best practices for managing large-scale

Kubernetes clusters, discuss strategies for maximizing uptime, and provide a practical guide to setting up a highly available Kubernetes cluster.

Cluster Management and Scaling: Managing Large-Scale Clusters

1. **Managing Large-Scale Clusters**:
   - As Kubernetes usage scales, managing a cluster becomes more complex. This includes monitoring resources, automating updates, ensuring security, and maintaining reliability.
   - **Best Practices**:
     - **Automated Monitoring and Logging**: Use tools like **Prometheus**, **Grafana**, and **ELK Stack** (Elasticsearch, Logstash, and Kibana) to monitor node performance, track application health, and identify potential issues.
     - **Resource Quotas and Limits**: Set quotas and resource limits to control resource usage across namespaces, ensuring fair allocation and preventing single workloads from over-consuming resources.
     - **Network and Security Policies**: Enforce security and network policies across

namespaces to secure applications and prevent unauthorized access.

2. **Cluster Scaling Strategies**:

    o   Kubernetes provides **horizontal and vertical scaling** mechanisms to meet varying workloads.

    o   **Horizontal Pod Autoscaler (HPA)**: Scales the number of pod replicas based on CPU or custom metrics, ensuring applications can handle increased load.

    o   **Cluster Autoscaler**: Automatically adjusts the number of nodes based on resource requirements. When pods cannot be scheduled due to insufficient resources, the Cluster Autoscaler adds nodes to the cluster.

    o   **Best Practices for Scaling**:

        ▪   **Define Scaling Thresholds**: Set CPU, memory, or custom metric thresholds that trigger autoscaling, allowing your cluster to adapt to changing demand.

        ▪   **Optimize for Cost and Performance**: Use autoscaling to scale down during low-traffic periods, reducing costs while maintaining performance during peak times.

3. **Multi-Cluster Management**:

- o In a production environment, you may want to manage multiple clusters across regions or cloud providers for enhanced resilience and compliance.
- o Tools like **KubeFed (Kubernetes Federation)** or **Rancher** enable centralized management of multiple clusters, allowing for unified policy control, monitoring, and application deployment.

Handling Node Failures and High Availability: Strategies for Ensuring Uptime

1. **Ensuring Node and Pod Resilience**:
   - o **Pod Disruption Budgets (PDB)**: Define minimum available or maximum unavailable pods for each application, ensuring that workloads remain available during disruptions.
   - o **Replica Sets**: Use multiple replicas to ensure that workloads are not impacted by individual pod failures. For critical applications, deploy replicas across nodes to prevent single-node failures from impacting availability.
2. **High Availability (HA) for Control Plane**:
   - o **Control Plane Redundancy**:
     - ▪ In a highly available setup, the control plane (API server, etcd, controller manager, and scheduler) is deployed across multiple nodes.

- **Load Balancer**: Place a load balancer in front of the control plane nodes to distribute traffic and ensure access to the API server if one node goes down.
- **HA for etcd**:
  - etcd stores the cluster's configuration and state; therefore, maintaining a highly available etcd is crucial. Deploy an odd number of etcd nodes (e.g., 3 or 5) across multiple availability zones for fault tolerance.
- **Disaster Recovery**:
  - Regularly back up etcd data to recover quickly from data loss or corruption.
  - Consider using automated backup tools and setting up recovery scripts to ensure rapid response to outages.

3. **Node Failure Strategies**:
   - **Node Pools**: Organize nodes into pools based on hardware specifications or application requirements. This helps manage workloads based on specific node capabilities (e.g., GPU, high-memory nodes).
   - **Automated Health Checks and Self-Healing**:
     - Use Kubernetes liveness and readiness probes to monitor pod health. Unhealthy

pods are automatically restarted, while readiness probes ensure that only healthy pods receive traffic.

- o **Monitoring and Alerting**:
    - Use alerting systems like Prometheus Alertmanager to detect node failures and automate responses, such as triggering an autoscaling event or notifying the DevOps team.

Example Scenario: A Guide to Setting Up a Highly Available Kubernetes Cluster

In this example, we'll walk through setting up a highly available Kubernetes cluster, focusing on making the control plane and etcd resilient and implementing strategies for node failure handling.

Scenario Overview

- We'll create a Kubernetes cluster with a highly available control plane across three nodes, configure etcd with redundancy, and ensure workloads can survive node failures using node pools, health checks, and autoscaling.
- This setup can be deployed on a cloud provider like AWS, GCP, or Azure, which typically offers multi-zone capabilities for high availability.

Step 1: Set Up Control Plane Nodes

1. **Provision Three Control Plane Nodes**:
   o Provision three nodes for the control plane in different availability zones to ensure that a failure in one zone doesn't impact cluster availability.

2. **Install Kubernetes Components**:
   o Install essential Kubernetes components (kube-apiserver, kube-scheduler, kube-controller-manager, and etcd) on each control plane node.

3. **Configure Load Balancer for API Server**:
   o Set up a load balancer in front of the API servers to distribute incoming requests.
   o Point client requests (e.g., kubectl, other nodes) to the load balancer's endpoint, which then routes traffic to available API servers.

4. **Configure etcd for High Availability**:
   o Deploy an odd number of etcd instances (e.g., 3 or 5) across control plane nodes to ensure fault tolerance.
   o Configure etcd instances with TLS for secure communication, and set up regular backups.

Step 2: Configure Node Pools for Workloads

1. **Create Node Pools for Different Workloads**:
   o Define node pools for various workload types:
     ▪ **Standard Node Pool**: For general-purpose applications.

- ▪ **High-Memory Node Pool**: For memory-intensive applications, such as databases.
- ▪ **GPU Node Pool**: For workloads requiring GPU processing.

2. **Apply Node Labels**:
   - ○ Label nodes in each pool based on their function (e.g., node-role.kubernetes.io/gpu=true), allowing applications to target specific nodes.

3. **Implement Node Affinity and Tolerations**:
   - ○ Use node affinity and tolerations to ensure that pods are scheduled on the appropriate nodes.
   - ○ Example: Use a toleration for pods that require high-memory nodes:

   yaml
   tolerations:
   - key: "high-memory"
     operator: "Equal"
     value: "true"
     effect: "NoSchedule"

Step 3: Enable Autoscaling and Self-Healing Mechanisms

1. **Configure Cluster Autoscaler**:
   - ○ Set up the Cluster Autoscaler to adjust the number of nodes in response to workload demands.

- o Enable the autoscaler with minimum and maximum limits for each node pool to control resource allocation and costs.

2. **Set Up Horizontal Pod Autoscaler (HPA)**:
   - o Define the HPA to scale pod replicas based on CPU or memory utilization:

```yaml
apiVersion: autoscaling/v2
kind: HorizontalPodAutoscaler
metadata:
  name: myapp-hpa
spec:
  scaleTargetRef:
    apiVersion: apps/v1
    kind: Deployment
    name: myapp
  minReplicas: 2
  maxReplicas: 10
  metrics:
  - type: Resource
    resource:
      name: cpu
      target:
        type: Utilization
        averageUtilization: 50
```

3. **Set Up Pod Disruption Budgets (PDB)**:
   - Use PDBs to ensure that a minimum number of replicas remain available during node disruptions:

```yaml
apiVersion: policy/v1
kind: PodDisruptionBudget
metadata:
  name: myapp-pdb
spec:
  minAvailable: 2
  selector:
    matchLabels:
      app: myapp
```

4. **Configure Liveness and Readiness Probes**:
   - Add liveness and readiness probes to detect unresponsive pods and remove them from service until healthy:

```yaml
Copy code
livenessProbe:
  httpGet:
    path: /health
    port: 8080
```

```
initialDelaySeconds: 10
periodSeconds: 5
readinessProbe:
  httpGet:
    path: /ready
    port: 8080
  initialDelaySeconds: 5
  periodSeconds: 5
```

Step 4: Set Up Monitoring, Alerting, and Disaster Recovery

1. **Install Monitoring and Logging Tools**:
   o Deploy **Prometheus** and **Grafana** to monitor cluster metrics, and set up alerts with Prometheus Alertmanager for critical events.
   o Use the **ELK Stack** (Elasticsearch, Logstash, and Kibana) to centralize and analyze logs from nodes and pods.

2. **Enable Disaster Recovery with etcd Backups**:
   o Set up a backup schedule for etcd using automated tools or scripts to ensure quick recovery if the control plane encounters issues.

3. **Define Alerting Rules for Node and Pod Failures**:
   o Configure alerting rules in Prometheus to notify the operations team of node failures, high resource

usage, or pod restarts, enabling a rapid response to issues.

In this chapter, we explored key strategies for running Kubernetes in production, focusing on **cluster management and scaling**, **handling node failures**, and **ensuring high availability**. We discussed scaling strategies with Cluster Autoscaler and HPA, handling node failures with Pod Disruption Budgets and automated health checks, and ensuring high availability with redundant control plane and etcd setups. Through a practical example, we demonstrated how to configure a highly available Kubernetes cluster with multi-zone control plane nodes, node pools for workload isolation, and monitoring and disaster recovery tools.

In the next chapter, we'll cover **Securing Kubernetes Workloads**, where we'll dive into security best practices to protect applications, control access, and secure sensitive data in a Kubernetes environment.

CHAPTER 19: KUBERNETES ON THE CLOUD

Running Kubernetes on the cloud has become the preferred choice for many organizations due to the availability of **managed Kubernetes services** and the scalability that cloud platforms offer. In this chapter, we'll explore popular managed Kubernetes services, discuss the key differences in cloud configurations for setting up and scaling, and walk through a practical example of deploying a multi-region application on a managed Kubernetes service.

Using Managed Kubernetes Services: Overview of GKE, EKS, and AKS

1. **What are Managed Kubernetes Services?**
   - Managed Kubernetes services simplify cluster deployment, management, and maintenance by handling much of the underlying infrastructure. They manage tasks like control plane setup, scaling, upgrades, and backups, allowing teams to focus on deploying and managing applications rather than the Kubernetes infrastructure itself.

2. **Popular Managed Kubernetes Services**:
   - **Google Kubernetes Engine (GKE)**:
     - GKE is Google Cloud's managed Kubernetes service, known for its seamless integration with other Google Cloud services and extensive support for multi-zone and multi-cluster deployments.
     - Key features: Autoscaling, private clusters, integrated monitoring, and release channels for controlled upgrades.
   - **Amazon Elastic Kubernetes Service (EKS)**:
     - EKS is AWS's managed Kubernetes service, providing high availability and integration with AWS services like IAM, RDS, and ALB.

- Key features: Enhanced security with IAM roles, VPC integration, Fargate support for serverless pods, and cluster autoscaler.
  - **Azure Kubernetes Service (AKS)**:
    - AKS is Microsoft Azure's managed Kubernetes offering, providing easy integration with Azure services and tools for scaling, monitoring, and managing applications.
    - Key features: Azure Active Directory integration, virtual node support with Azure Container Instances, and integrated monitoring with Azure Monitor.

3. **Benefits of Using Managed Kubernetes Services**:
   - **Reduced Operational Complexity**: Managed services handle tasks like control plane maintenance, upgrades, and scaling, freeing teams to focus on application development.
   - **Cost Optimization**: Cloud providers offer autoscaling to dynamically adjust resources, reducing costs during periods of low demand.
   - **Enhanced Security and Compliance**: Managed services include built-in security controls, compliance certifications, and monitoring tools.

Setting Up and Scaling in the Cloud: Differences in Cloud Configurations

1. **Control Plane and Node Management**:
   - **Control Plane**: Managed services handle the control plane, so users do not manage or scale control plane nodes directly. Control planes are typically distributed across availability zones for high availability.
   - **Node Pools**: Managed services allow users to define node pools with varying machine types, operating systems, and zones. Different node pools can be used to separate workloads based on their resource requirements or geographic locations.

2. **Autoscaling Options**:
   - **Cluster Autoscaler**: Most managed services include a cluster autoscaler that adds or removes nodes based on resource demand. This can be configured to scale specific node pools within a single region or across multiple zones.
   - **Horizontal Pod Autoscaler (HPA)**: Supported on all managed services, the HPA adjusts the number of pod replicas based on metrics like CPU or memory usage.
   - **Fargate (EKS)** and **Virtual Nodes (AKS)**: AWS and Azure provide serverless options (Fargate for

EKS and Virtual Nodes for AKS) that allow pods to run without provisioning fixed nodes, which is particularly useful for burstable workloads.

3. **Networking and Load Balancing**:
   - Each cloud provider has a unique approach to networking, including VPCs in AWS, VNet in Azure, and Google's Virtual Private Cloud. These configurations control how network traffic flows to and from the cluster.
   - **Load Balancers**:
     - Managed services automatically provision cloud load balancers for services configured with LoadBalancer type, distributing traffic across nodes and ensuring high availability.
     - **Ingress Controllers**: GKE, EKS, and AKS offer support for managed ingress controllers, with options for integrating with cloud-native load balancers (such as AWS ALB or Google's Global Load Balancer).

4. **Storage Options**:
   - Managed services integrate with native storage solutions such as **Amazon EBS** for EKS, **Azure Disks** for AKS, and **Google Persistent Disks** for GKE. These storage options support persistent

volumes that can be dynamically provisioned and attached to pods.

- o **Multi-Region Storage**: For applications requiring redundancy across regions, consider using managed databases or storage services like AWS RDS, Azure Cosmos DB, or Google Cloud Spanner.

Practical Example: Deploying a Multi-Region Application on a Managed Kubernetes Service

In this example, we'll deploy a web application on Google Kubernetes Engine (GKE) with a multi-region setup, enabling the application to serve traffic from multiple regions for high availability and low latency.

Scenario Overview

- Deploy a simple web application with an NGINX front end in multiple regions.
- Use Google's multi-regional load balancer to route traffic to the closest region based on user location.
- Configure autoscaling to handle varying workloads across regions.

Step 1: Set Up GKE Clusters in Multiple Regions

1. **Create GKE Clusters in Two Regions**:

o Choose two regions (e.g., us-central1 and europe-west1) and create a cluster in each region:

bash

gcloud container clusters create cluster-us \
  --region us-central1 \
  --num-nodes 3 \
  --enable-autoscaling --min-nodes 1 --max-nodes 5

gcloud container clusters create cluster-eu \
  --region europe-west1 \
  --num-nodes 3 \
  --enable-autoscaling --min-nodes 1 --max-nodes 5

2. **Verify Cluster Creation**:
   o Ensure both clusters are created successfully:

bash

gcloud container clusters list

Step 2: Deploy the Application to Each Cluster

1. **Configure kubectl Contexts**:
   o Set the kubectl context to the us-central1 cluster and deploy the application:

bash

Copy code

gcloud container clusters get-credentials cluster-us --region us-central1

2. **Deploy the Application**:
   ○ Create a deployment for an NGINX application in cluster-us:

   yaml
   Copy code

```yaml
apiVersion: apps/v1
kind: Deployment
metadata:
  name: web-app
spec:
  replicas: 3
  selector:
    matchLabels:
      app: web-app
  template:
    metadata:
      labels:
        app: web-app
    spec:
      containers:
      - name: nginx
```

```
image: nginx:latest
ports:
- containerPort: 80
```

   o   Apply the deployment:

```
bash
kubectl apply -f web-app-deployment.yaml
```

3. **Expose the Application with a Service**:

   o   Expose the application as a LoadBalancer service in each cluster:

```yaml
yaml
Copy code
apiVersion: v1
kind: Service
metadata:
  name: web-app-service
spec:
  type: LoadBalancer
  selector:
    app: web-app
  ports:
  - protocol: TCP
    port: 80
    targetPort: 80
```

o Apply the service configuration:

bash
kubectl apply -f web-app-service.yaml

4. **Repeat Steps for the Europe Cluster**:
    o Switch to the Europe cluster context, deploy the application, and expose it using the same configurations.

Step 3: Configure a Global Load Balancer in Google Cloud

1. **Obtain the External IP Addresses**:
    o For each region's web-app-service, retrieve the external IP addresses:

bash
Copy code
kubectl get svc web-app-service

2. **Set Up Google's Global Load Balancer**:
    o In the Google Cloud Console, configure a global load balancer using **Cloud Load Balancing**. Add the external IP addresses of both regional clusters as backend services.

3. **Configure Traffic Routing**:

o Set up routing rules in the load balancer to direct user traffic based on geographic proximity, ensuring that users connect to the closest available region for low-latency access.

4. **Set Up Health Checks**:

o Configure health checks on the load balancer to monitor each backend service, ensuring that traffic is routed only to healthy instances.

Step 4: Test and Verify Multi-Region Deployment

1. **Test Application Access**:

o Access the application through the global load balancer's IP address or DNS name. The load balancer should route requests to the closest regional cluster based on the user's location.

2. **Monitor Autoscaling and Load Balancer Health**:

o Monitor the autoscaling activity in each GKE cluster to confirm that the clusters respond to varying load.

o Check load balancer logs and health check statuses to ensure the application remains available in both regions.

3. **Simulate Failover**:

o Test failover by temporarily disabling the application in one region. The load balancer should automatically route traffic to the available region, demonstrating resilience in the multi-region setup.

In this chapter, we discussed deploying Kubernetes on the cloud using **managed Kubernetes services** like GKE, EKS, and AKS. These services simplify Kubernetes operations by managing tasks like scaling, security, and high availability. We explored differences in cloud configurations, including autoscaling options, network and load balancing, and storage integration. Through a practical example, we deployed a multi-region application on GKE, configuring a global load balancer to route traffic based on geographic location and implementing autoscaling to handle dynamic workloads.

In the next chapter, we'll cover **Kubernetes Security and Compliance**, where we'll dive deeper into securing Kubernetes environments and meeting compliance requirements

CHAPTER 20: KUBERNETES BEST PRACTICES AND THE FUTURE

As we conclude our journey through Kubernetes, this chapter will review best practices for efficient Kubernetes management, explore emerging trends, and provide a look at the future of Kubernetes in hybrid and multi-cloud environments. We'll also share resources for advanced topics, helping you continue your learning journey.

Review of Best Practices: Summing Up Tips for Efficient Kubernetes Management

1. **Cluster Management and Resource Optimization**:
   o **Use Namespaces**: Organize resources and enforce boundaries between teams or environments (e.g., dev, test, production) with namespaces.
   o **Resource Quotas and Limits**: Set quotas and resource limits to control resource usage per namespace and prevent resource hogging.
   o **Autoscaling**: Leverage the **Horizontal Pod Autoscaler** and **Cluster Autoscaler** to dynamically adjust resources, keeping costs optimized and applications responsive to traffic spikes.
2. **Networking and Load Balancing**:

- o **Network Policies**: Secure pod communication by restricting traffic flow using network policies, ensuring that only approved services can interact.

- o **Ingress Controllers and Load Balancing**: Set up ingress controllers for efficient routing of external traffic. Use load balancers to distribute traffic across replicas and regions for high availability.

- o **Multi-Region and Multi-Availability Zone Deployments**: Distribute your workloads across multiple zones or regions for resilience and failover support.

3. **Storage and Data Management**:

- o **Persistent Volumes and Storage Classes**: Standardize storage for stateful applications using persistent volumes and storage classes, which allows for consistent and reliable data storage.

- o **Backup and Disaster Recovery**: Regularly back up data in persistent storage and use automated disaster recovery procedures for critical workloads to minimize downtime during failures.

4. **Security and Compliance**:

- o **Role-Based Access Control (RBAC)**: Apply the principle of least privilege by assigning specific permissions to users, groups, or service accounts.

- o **Pod Security Standards**: Enforce security practices like running containers as non-root users, using read-only filesystems, and limiting container privileges.
- o **Secrets Management**: Use Kubernetes secrets to store sensitive information securely, and consider external secret management solutions for added security.
- o **Audit Logs**: Enable audit logging to track changes and access patterns within the cluster, aiding in compliance and security investigations.

5. **Monitoring, Logging, and Troubleshooting**:
   - o **Centralized Monitoring**: Use tools like Prometheus, Grafana, and ELK Stack for centralized monitoring, alerting, and log analysis.
   - o **Health Checks and Self-Healing**: Implement liveness and readiness probes to ensure application health, allowing Kubernetes to replace or route around failed pods.
   - o **Pod Disruption Budgets**: Set Pod Disruption Budgets (PDBs) to maintain availability during node maintenance or upgrades.

Emerging Trends and Future of Kubernetes: Exploring the Role of Kubernetes in Hybrid and Multi-Cloud Setups

1. **Hybrid and Multi-Cloud Kubernetes**:
   - ○ Many organizations are adopting **hybrid** (on-premises and cloud) or **multi-cloud** (multiple cloud providers) setups for improved resilience, reduced vendor lock-in, and optimized costs.
   - ○ **Tools Supporting Multi-Cloud Kubernetes**:
     - ▪ **KubeFed (Kubernetes Federation)**: Enables management of multiple clusters from a central control plane, streamlining operations in multi-cloud environments.
     - ▪ **Crossplane**: Extends Kubernetes with cloud service abstractions, enabling seamless management of resources across AWS, GCP, and Azure from within Kubernetes.
     - ▪ **Service Meshes (Istio, Linkerd)**: Service meshes manage cross-cluster traffic, observability, and security, facilitating application communication across multiple environments.

2. **Serverless and Kubernetes**:
   - ○ Kubernetes now supports **serverless workloads** through integrations with tools like **Knative** and managed container services such as AWS Fargate (for EKS) and Google Cloud Run (for Anthos).

o These tools allow you to run containers without managing nodes, which reduces operational overhead for unpredictable or bursty workloads.

3. **Edge Computing**:

o As **edge computing** grows, Kubernetes is increasingly being deployed on edge devices or distributed across edge locations.

o **K3s and MicroK8s**: These lightweight Kubernetes distributions are designed for edge environments, supporting IoT, smart cities, and remote deployments with limited resources.

4. **Artificial Intelligence and Machine Learning (AI/ML) on Kubernetes**:

o Kubernetes has become a popular platform for deploying AI and ML workloads due to its support for GPU scheduling, custom resources, and scalable computing environments.

o Tools like **Kubeflow** provide an end-to-end machine learning pipeline on Kubernetes, allowing teams to develop, train, and deploy ML models in a consistent, scalable way.

5. **Automation and GitOps**:

o **GitOps** has emerged as a best practice for managing Kubernetes environments, treating Git as the single source of truth for infrastructure configurations.

- o Tools like **Argo CD** and **Flux** automate deployment and configuration management, providing a clear audit trail, consistency, and rollback capabilities through Git.

Final Thoughts and Next Steps: Where to Go from Here and Resources for Advanced Kubernetes Topics

1. **Mastering Advanced Kubernetes Topics**:
   - o As you become more comfortable with Kubernetes basics, consider diving into advanced areas like **service mesh deployment**, **multi-cluster management**, **GitOps workflows**, and **Kubernetes Operator** development.
   - o **Recommended Learning Pathways**:
     - ▪ **Kubernetes Operators**: Explore how to build and use operators for automating complex application lifecycles. Operators encapsulate domain knowledge, making it easier to deploy and manage applications like databases and AI platforms.
     - ▪ **Service Meshes (e.g., Istio)**: Learn how to implement a service mesh to manage

microservices communication, security, and observability within your applications.

- **Kubernetes Security**: Focus on enhancing cluster security through advanced topics like Pod Security Policies, OPA/Gatekeeper for policy enforcement, and runtime security tools.

2. **Further Resources and Communities**:

   o **Books and Documentation**:

     - *Kubernetes Up and Running* by Kelsey Hightower, Brendan Burns, and Joe Beda – A comprehensive guide to Kubernetes with practical examples.

     - Kubernetes official documentation (https://kubernetes.io/docs/) – A valuable resource with in-depth guides, best practices, and tutorials.

   o **Certifications**:

     - Consider certifications such as **Certified Kubernetes Administrator (CKA)** and **Certified Kubernetes Application Developer (CKAD)** to validate your expertise.

   o **Communities and Events**:

- Engage with the Kubernetes community by participating in events like **KubeCon** and joining forums like the **Kubernetes Slack** and **CNCF Community**. These platforms are great for networking, sharing knowledge, and staying updated with Kubernetes advancements.

3. **Experimenting with Advanced Tools and Setups**:
    o Practice implementing CI/CD pipelines, service meshes, and multi-cluster setups on sandbox environments or cloud providers.
    o Explore tools like **Rancher** for multi-cluster management, **Kubeflow** for machine learning pipelines, and **Crossplane** for cloud-native resource management.

In this chapter, we reviewed best practices for efficient Kubernetes management, including recommendations for cluster management, security, scaling, and monitoring. We explored emerging trends such as hybrid and multi-cloud Kubernetes, serverless workloads, edge computing, and GitOps, highlighting how Kubernetes is shaping the future of infrastructure. Finally, we provided guidance on advanced topics, resources for continued learning, and tips for engaging with the Kubernetes community.

As you move forward, remember that Kubernetes is constantly evolving, with new tools, practices, and use cases emerging regularly. Stay curious, keep experimenting, and continue building your skills to unlock the full potential of Kubernetes in production environments. This journey will empower you to architect resilient, scalable, and efficient cloud-native applications that meet the demands of the future.

www.ingramcontent.com/pod-product-compliance
Lightning Source LLC
LaVergne TN
LVHW051445050326
832903LV00030BD/3249